C000099895

Liturgical Re~~vision in~~

the Church of England

1984-2004:

The working of
the Liturgical Commission

by
David Hebblethwaite OBE BA
Secretary to the Commission 1984-2004

GROVE BOOKS LIMITED
RIDLEY HALL RD CAMBRIDGE CB3 9HU

Contents

1 From Cranmer to Common Worship 3

2 Framework and agenda 6

3 Advent to Advent 9

4 From Directory to Office 11

5 From background to foreground: some issues 20

6 From Cradle to Grave 26

7 Eucharist and Ministry 33

   Appendix: Membership of the Liturgical Commission from 1981 45

Copyright David Hebblethwaite, 2004

Introduction

This Study is taken from a much longer first draft. Its constructive abridgement (and the arrangement of its sections) has been undertaken by Trevor Lloyd to bring the text into the confines of an Alcuin/GROW Study. Even the longer version was largely confined to the workings of the Liturgical Commission and made no attempt to précis published documents detailing other significant input to liturgical revision from the processes in General Synod. References to the published documents are included here, though access to them becomes increasingly difficult. The parallel process of liturgical publishing deserves its own study and is not included here. Quotations from the Commission's minutes are made with the goodwill of my successor as secretary, Dr. Colin Podmore, and the text could not have emerged without the help of the Commission's administrative assistant, Sue Moore. It is my hope that the extensive records of liturgical change will soon be available to serious researchers, who will find that the present Study is no more than an *hors d'oeuvre*.

THE COVER PICTURE

is a photo of a selection of the liturgical publications the origins of which form the theme of the Study.

First Impression October 2004

ISSN 0951-2667

ISBN 1 85174 571 8

1
From Cranmer to Common Worship

The story of liturgical change in the Church of England from the days of Cranmer to the Alternative Service Book is told in many other places. This present Study takes the story from 1984 to 2004, to a point where the revision, refinement and expansion of the ASB's provisions were authorized, published and in use as *Common Worship*.[1]

The processes of change have themselves changed over the years. From 1549 to 1966 changes required the assent of Parliament, and Parliament is a lay voice. After 1662 there was a long period when no changes were made. When in 1919-20 new machinery was devised for the Church Assembly to send legislation (known as Measures) to Parliament, Parliament rejected the 'Deposited Book' in 1927 and 1928.

Since the Church of England (Alternative and Other Services) Measure 1965 and the Church of England (Worship and Doctrine) Measure 1974 full power has been devolved from Parliament first to the Church Assembly and, since 1970, to the General Synod, to authorize 'alternative services' by two-thirds majorities in each of the three Houses of Synod. This dynamic combination of clerical Convocations and the crucially important House of Laity is governed by standing orders which ensure that every opportunity is given to members to amend the text of liturgical proposals, and each text comes before Synod at least three times for debate prior to authorization—a process designed to secure 'ownership' of the new liturgy by all sections in the Church – a *sensus fidelium*. Such consent gives new liturgy a status equal to that of the sixteenth and seventeenth century texts in reflecting the Church of England's belief and position to outside enquirers

There are two qualifications to this pattern of authorization which bear on changes in the liturgy:

First, the authorized texts include not only alternatives and options, but also considerable space for local choice and preferences (whether in hymns, prayers, or linking material).

Second, the texts which require such authorization are 'alternative' to actual services in the 1662 Book of Common Prayer. Other services may be used at the discretion of the officiant. The House of Bishops has devised since 1985 a process of 'commending' services (see page 5).

The upshot is that, although there are official printed books and electronic texts of Common Worship, parishes have freedom to provide their own congregational booklets, or texts on screen. Adherence and loyalty to the central

---

1   See also by this publisher Colin Buchanan's *Recent Liturgical Revision in the Church of England to 1973* (1973); *Recent Liturgical Revision in the Church of England: Supplement for 1973-74* (1974); *Recent Liturgical Revision in the Church of England: Supplement for 1974-76* (1976); *Recent Liturgical Revision in the Church of England: Supplement for 1976-78* (1978); *Latest Liturgical Revision in the Church of England 1978-1984* (1984). These (numbered 14, 14a, 14b, 14c in the Grove Ministry and Worship Series and 39 in the Grove Liturgical Studies) provide a detailed record.

or 'core' texts representing the doctrinal and worshipping stance of the Church of England is the basis for a continuing Anglican ethos within the myriad of local variations.

Prior to 1981

The Liturgical Commission was first formed in 1955 and from 1965 brought forward a steady stream of proposals for liturgical reform. Series One services were produced by the House of Bishops to legalize 1928 texts already in widespread use. The Commission's Series Two proposals were truly experimental, and were followed from 1971 by Series Three which made the cultural (if not liturgical) advance of addressing God in contemporary English. All of these were time-limited trials (though all required two-thirds majorities in each House of Synod). The later of them (Calendar and Lectionary, Initiation, Marriage, Ordinal) were taken forward with renewed mandate after 1980. The earliest (Holy Communion) was revised in the light of experience, first in 'traditional language' ('Series One and Two Revised', later Rite B) and (from 1977) in Rite A. When the Worship and Doctrine Measure passed into law in 1975, the Synod decided on a longer-term single book. The revision of Series Three communion became Rite A as the centre-piece of the new book.[2] The *Alternative Service Book* was published on 10 November 1980.

Authorization was for ten years only, a term which could only be extended (by a process requiring two-thirds majorities in all three Houses) if it remained unaltered in every detail. Small textual changes would have involved major synodical procedures and considerable local disaffection. Permission for parishes to make locally adapted booklets for their own use, though deferred for commercial reasons, was available two years after publication. The Liturgical Commission of 1981-86 delayed any assessment of how the book was being received, and instead began to supplement the book. In their 'end-of-term' report, *The Worship of the Church* (GS 698, 1985), they acknowledged the need for a critical new look at ASB texts. The Standing Committee of General Synod realised that this would need a further extension of the ten-year period of licence. The new Synod, elected in 1985, duly extended authorization from 31 December 1990 to 31 December 2000.

1981 – 1986

The Commission of 1976-81 had completed some work which had not been included in the ASB. Three draft services were published in late 1980: Ministry

---

2   This latter was by far the most thorough-going process in the 1970s. It involved a six-month parley between the Liturgical Commission and the House of Bishops before proposals reached the Synod (this parley concerned the wording of anamnesis in eucharistic prayer), and then a prolonged and massively-detailed revision in committee (for which the present author was minute-taker) and at significant points further revision on the floor of the whole Synod, taking 19 hours in full Synod.

to the Sick, Reconciliation of a Penitent, and the Blessing of Oils. Ministry to the Sick was authorized in November 1982, but the other two failed to achieve two-thirds majorities in the House of Laity.[3]

A major task for the Commission in the 1981-86 period was new ground, the preparation of services for *Lent, Holy Week, Easter*, to enrich the mainstream liturgy in the period between Ash Wednesday and Pentecost. There existed widespread variant practices ranging from the wholesale borrowing of Roman Catholic provision to less structured devotional services or the addition of symbol (as, e.g., the distribution of palm crosses). The Commission was able to find uncontroversial recommendations, but was in need of a procedure for promoting their use. As the material was deemed to lie outside anything strictly 'alternative' to services in the 1662 book, any officiant might (under canon B5) arguably use whatever rites were thought appropriate—but if Synod, Convocation or individual bishops claimed to 'authorize' any such rites, they would by the same token be banning other uses and removing discretion from individual ministers. The way through was found by the House of Bishops 'commending'.[4] A Synod debate was held in 1985, and the services were commended in January 1986, in time for use that year.[5]

3   A legal opinion had ruled that 'reconciliation of a penitent' was essentially 'alternative' to part of the Book of Common Prayer *Visitation of the Sick* and therefore needed full synodical authorization. That legal opinion has recently (2003) been revised.
4   See page 6 overleaf.
5   The Commission took steps to 'road test' its draft rites (using a congregation at Addington where it was meeting) and also 'launched' the rites in a residential conference for diocesan representatives. This became the pattern for the end of each successive five-year period thereafter.

2
Framework and agenda

From 1986 onwards, liturgical revision has functioned within a well structured framework of synodical bodies and processes. Some of this framework has already emerged in the summary of events pre-1986, but it will help an understanding of particular themes if it is laid out more fully.

The Liturgical Commission
New Commissions are formed with each new Synod, the members being appointed by the Archbishops after consultation with the Standing Committee of Synod (since 1998 the Appointments Committee for the Church of England). Thus there have been Commissions for 1986-91, 1991-96, 1996-2001, and, at the time of writing, the Commission of 2001-6 is at work[6]. From 1986 the chairman was Bishop Colin James, of Winchester; he continued till 1993, and was succeeded that year by David Stancliffe, about to be Bishop of Salisbury. (It has been announced that he will be succeeded in 2005 by Bishop Stephen Platten, of Wakefield.) The Commission receives its instructions from the House of Bishops (though it sometimes suggests priorities to the House), and business only comes before Synod by *fiat* of that House. Commission members are not all members of General Synod, but it is a requirement that a good proportion of them are, since they are needed for the complex synodical work which follows the Commission's drafting.

The Commission holds an annual information-sharing day with diocesan representatives, and at the end of each quinquennium follows the 1985 precedent by hosting a residential conference for the dioceses, and at this rites are introduced by the actual use of them.

The General Synod
In the period from 1986 General Synod has handled liturgical drafts in two different ways, according to the nature of the material.

First, there is the 'commended' approach, pioneered for *Lent, Holy Week, Easter*, and used for giving some official standing to liturgical material which is not 'alternative' to anything in the 1662 BCP. The procedures for this do not arise from the canons or the Synod's standing orders, but are simply a working *ad hoc* arrangement. The Commission brings texts to the House of Bishops, they are then debated in General Synod once (on a 'take note' basis, which does not allow for amending), and they then return to the Commission for amendment in the light of debate. They then go to the House of Bishops and are published with the House's 'commendation'.

---

6   For details of the membership in each quinquennium see the Appendix on pp 45-46.

Second, there is the 'authorization' procedure, for services which are 'alternative' to those in the BCP. The Worship and Doctrine Measure 1974 requires a two-thirds majority in each of the three Houses of Synod for such authorization. General Synod itself devises Standing Orders to ensure the fullest possible support for such services when they come to the final vote. During the period of this Study, the procedure has been:

1. A first debate—the text then goes a revision committee.

2. The revision committee (having received submissions and interviewed those who wish to plead in person for their proposals) takes a revised text to Synod, with a Report covering every submission made.

3. The revision stage in Synod follows, at which members may refer specified parts of the text back to the revision committee. If no reference back occurs, the text is deemed acceptable to the Synod, and returns to the House of Bishops (see 5 below).

4. If any part is referred back, the revision committee reports to a second revision stage in full Synod. This time members may move specific textual amendments before it returns to the House of Bishops.

5. The House of Bishops has responsibility for determining the final form of the text, but uses this power carefully.[7]

6. The final form comes to the Synod for final approval by two-thirds majorities in each House.

The agenda

The chronological framework of the period was the twenty-year life of the ASB.[8] Unless extensions of time were to be given to individual services[9], replacement rites needed to be authorized well before the deadline at the end of the year 2000. The earlier part of the period included a high proportion of material for commendation, while services for full authorization were handled at an early drafting stage in the Commission. Process in General Synod needed to be almost entirely within the quinquennium 1995-2000. (It was desirable that the synodical stages should not run across an election to General Synod). Timetabling of the processes of assent by the House of Bishops and debating, revising and authorizing in Synod was of crucial importance.

This was the background when the new Liturgical Commission met in March 1986 under Bishop Colin James. The headings in the minutes of that meeting

---

7   This caution goes back to 1978 when the House restored Josephine Butler (whom the Synod had earlier rejected by a tiny margin) to the calendar by 22 votes to 21, and thus precipitated a storm of frustration in the Synod, which could not further amend the text, but could hardly defeat a whole calendar and lectionary over one tiny issue.

8   Originally, this had been for ten years, but an initial decision of the 1985-1990 Synod was to extend the ASB's time to 31 December 2000.

9   Eg the ordinal (see page 43)

adumbrate the whole agenda of the ensuing fifteen years. They are:

(a) The proposal for a 'directory';

(b) Degrees of authorization [ie 'authorized' and 'commended'];

(c) Prayer Book and Series One issues;

(d) Inclusive language;

(e) Local adaptation and experimentation;

(f) Doctrinal issues;

(g) Initiation;

(h) A fresh look at the Office and lectionary;

(i) 'Family Service' issues [including simplified credal statements]

(j) Work on liturgy for Advent to Candlemas

(k) More generally, the overall revision of ASB (including its mainstream rites) by 2000.

(l) A strong recognition that liturgical work should be undertaken with maximum regard for 'outside' input from diocesan liturgical committees, other groups (eg UPA[10] needs) and observers from other traditions.

In preparation for the tasks ahead the Commission set up a sub–group on catechesis and evangelism in worship (in conjunction with a visit of some members to the Institute for Pastoral Liturgy at Carlow in Ireland) to address the special requirements of UPAs and to assess failings in addressing these concerns. Another sub-group began early moves towards the production of a resource for *Advent to Candlemas*.

---

10 Urban Priority Areas, a phrase popularized by the publication in December 1985 of *Faith in the City* (Church House Publishing), the report of the Arcbishops' Commission on 'Urban Priority Areas'.

3
Advent to Advent

The Promise of His Glory

One main work of the 1986–1991 Commission was the provision of seasonal material for the period from All Saints' Day (1 November)[11] to the Presentation of Christ in the Temple (2 February), parallel to *Lent, Holy Week, Easter*. But, whereas *Lent, Holy Week, Easter* had been regularizing widely used and traditional customs such as the use of palms, ashes and a Paschal Candle, the new period had few ancient associations, though there were more recent 'traditions' of carol services, the Advent wreath, the Christingle and Remembrancetide. The result is more a collection of resources than prescribed rites and the 'evocative' rather than 'functional' title (*The Promise of His Glory*) reflects this.

As work progressed it included emerging views within the Commission on the future pattern for Calendar and (Sunday) Lectionary and it was also closely linked to the emerging proposals for *Patterns for Worship*. Individual members wrote essays on aspects of the subject for discussion in March 1987. The Commission recognized some of the problems: the secular celebration of Christmas (with ever more protracted anticipation of the actual festival); the popularity of any service 'by candlelight', coupled with lack of imagination in using the popular themes of darkness and light; the intrusion of Bible Sunday in any thought–out lead–up to Christmas. 'The co–operation of the Bible Society would be crucial'. Teams of members worked on drafts which were brought to the full Commission by September 1987. In March 1988 discussion focussed on 'the Communion of Saints in the Evangelical tradition' as one of the issues around All Saints/All Souls, an early engagement with the issues which would arise in revising funeral services.

The inclusion of lectionary and psalter tables was a conscious 'kite–flying' towards the emerging proposals for Calendar and Lectionary in the following decade, but it was made clear that they were not authorized for use. As with *Lent, Holy Week, Easter* there was Synod debate on the proposals (July 1990), the text was revised by the Commission, commended by the House of Bishops and published, though not in time for Advent 1990. As in 1985, the text was launched at a national residential conference in September 1990.

Times and Seasons

The 1991–1996 Commission recognized the need to bring together the seasonal compilations (*Lent, Holy Week, Easter* ,and *The Promise of His Glory* together with a private enterprise volume, *Enriching the Christian Year*) and to conform them to the emerging style of *Common Worship*.

---

11   The original starting point (Advent) was early moved back to 1 November.

Once the Commission's proposals for the calendar and lectionary had been agreed and taken to General Synod (July 1995), and Synod had accepted that the publication of revised liturgy in 2000 would be in a series of volumes rather than in one book (July 1996), work began on *Times and Seasons* material. A sub-group was set up at the beginning of the 1996–2001 Commission and has worked continuously since then, though with a major change of membership from 2000. Drafts were debated in General Synod in July 2004, with a view to commendation and publication in 2005.

4
From Directory to Office

The 'Directory'

The 1985 Report *The Worship of the Church* (GS 698) talked of the need for a 'Directory', a word used in two quite distinct senses. There was need for a book of 'best practice' showing how existing liturgical resources could be effectively used, which naturally led towards providing a bank of suitable resources. It was also perceived by 1986 that the successor to ASB might have more of the character of a directory, leaving much wider scope for local initiatives within laid–down guidelines and 'key' texts. (This eventually led to the production of *A Service of the Word* allied to a relatively wide choice of authorized texts for such 'key' elements as penitence and affirmation of faith.) The 1986–1991 Commission consulted the House of Bishops (June 1986) about its proposed programme of work and one concern was that Prayer Book and Series One issues should be included in the Commission's work so as to make a more flexible use of traditional language texts possible. Questions asked at the July 1986 General Synod and the meeting with diocesan liturgical representatives that autumn indicated that the Commission should include issues connected with 'family' services and the Offices in a coordinated approach to non–eucharistic Sunday worship.

By March 1987 a sub–group of Commission members had identified key issues around the concept of a 'Directory'. The ASB was found too restrictive in many pastoral situations: where Sunday worship was non–eucharistic, should the underlying 'shape' be from 'The Liturgy of the Word' or 'Morning Prayer'? There would also be sensitivity over allowing alternatives to the Nicene Creed — and to the eucharistic prayer where freer forms of Sunday worship were eucharistic. Requests from urban priority areas and from the more suburban 'family service' culture were fundamentally similar requests to adapt liturgy to meet local pastoral circumstance, which the Commission detected might be met by one rubrical structure. It was also agreed that any publication ought to include explicit guidance on 'presentation' issues and worked–out sample services. It was evident that, to allow such flexibility (moving further than had so far been found acceptable for authorized services), the 'commendation' route already established for *Lent, Holy Week, Easter* would have to be used.

As a background to this work, consultations in selected UPA parishes across the country were organized for Spring 1988, and the first of three consultations with chaplains in ministry to deaf people also took place. A further category of need was highlighted in early 1988, when *Children in the Way* (National Society/ CHP 1988) made specific request of the Commission to incorporate 'child–friendly' material.

By early 1988 the Commission's sub–group had produced a large corpus of resource material for inclusion in a commended publication, but it was apparent that if this was to be received and used as intended, more general and discursive reflections would be required on such issues as the 'balance' to be observed between statutory authorized services and these freer forms of worship, as well as on such topics as the meaning of 'family' in a liturgical context and the dangers of over–emphasis on such services.

The Commission distinguished between a few sensitive points where a common mind was essential if common prayer was to be preserved (for instance in eucharistic prayers), and a clear and accepted framework within which a wide variety of material (not all of which would need to have come from the Commission or have been synodically approved), could be inserted to suit local circumstance.

Early in 1989 the House of Bishops had its first opportunity to react to the emerging proposals. The work by now included guidance and resources for non–eucharistic acts of worship and draft texts for (doctrinally–sensitive) confession, absolution, affirmation of faith and eucharistic prayers. Four draft eucharistic prayers had emerged in the Commission's discussions, attempting varied approaches to the perceived problem of theological 'jargon' in the lengthy prayers in the ASB. The Commission persuaded the bishops to allow all this work to go to Synod for debate in February 1990 and to postpone questions of formal authorization for those parts which would need such a process (eg eucharistic prayers) until a new Synod had been elected in November 1990. The 'report edition' of *Patterns for Worship* (a name devised early in 1989) was published at the end of November 1989. This plain grey paper–covered publication (GS 898) was never commended or given any authorized status, but rapidly sold out and the accompanying pack of illustrative service cards soon passed into widespread use in parishes across the land. One strategy employed was the publication (as GS Misc 333) of a commentary on the rationale behind the draft eucharistic prayers in *Patterns for Worship* by two members of the Commission (Kenneth Stevenson and Bryan Spinks). The Commission itself provided background for the next stages of this work in its 1990 'end of term' report *The Worship of the Church as it approaches the Third Millennium* (GS Misc 364).

The Commission of 1986–1991 intended that its successor should press on quickly towards authorization or commendation of *Patterns for Worship*. Early in the life of the new Commission, however, the decision was taken to split the contents of the 1989 report edition into three sections

(a) A Service of the Word, with penitential and credal material, for synodical authorization;

(b) the eucharistic proposals (at that stage called 'Rite C'), also requiring a Synod process; and

(c) commended resource material for use in any context allowed by the rubrics.

The House of Bishops, asked in June 1992 to support this proposed division of *Patterns for Worship*, decided to hold back the eucharistic proposals until they could form part of a larger revision of the ASB eucharistic rites. The Synod authorization process for *A Service of the Word* including *Prayers of Penitence* with *Affirmations of Faith* began in February 1993. At that stage it was still envisaged that the resource material would be published before synodical authorization for *A Service of the*

Word could be obtained. In practice, difficulties over publication (including a late withdrawal of prospective joint publishers from the project) meant that the fully authorized *A Service of the Word with Affirmations of Faith and Prayers of Penitence* was available for a year *before* its publication as part of *Patterns for Worship* in July 1995. In the meantime some difficult decisions had to be taken by the Commission, eg whether the Canticles in *Patterns for Worship* should conform to the text accepted in 1980 (an ICET text in the case of Gospel Canticles) or follow the ELLC[12] texts which were being proposed for the next round of liturgical authorization. In the event it was decided to stick with the 1980 texts until revision of the ASB.[13]

When the drafts accompanied by explanatory notes from the Liturgical Commission (GS 1037 and GS 1038) were circulated to the Synod for February 1993, there was no certainty that they would be well received. They were introduced by Trevor Lloyd, a member of the Commission much involved in the initial drafting. In fact the Revision Committee, chaired by Mr Timothy Belben, reported by July and Final Approval was given in November 1993.

The principal part of the provision was radical, not a full service to use instead of Morning or Evening Prayer (like the various forms of 'Family Service' in widespread use), rather a 'recipe' of necessary and mandatory elements which should be included in a service, the actual texts to be drawn from other resources to meet local needs. This outline order was preceded by a prose explanatory introduction which was *included* in the text to be authorized and thus enjoyed as much authority as the outline order itself. It was now the case that, with full synodical authorization, any locally–devised form of service which included the mandatory elements, and used authorized texts where stipulated, was a fully–authorized alternative to BCP Morning or Evening Prayer. Although the provision was initially aimed at the growing 'family service' constituency, it was deliberately not tied to such occasions; even the most formal and traditional of liturgies *could* qualify; the novelty was to leave the precise form of service to local initiative, something which was already happening in practice on a wide scale, but was not legally fulfilling the requirement of the Canons unless Morning and/or Evening Prayer were used in addition.

The forms of penitence and Affirmations of Faith in GS 1037 and GS 1038 gave authorized status to a wide range of confessions and absolutions and to the possibility of 'Kyrie' confessions, as well as some scriptural affirmations of faith which might sometimes replace the Creed at main Sunday services.

12   The English Language Liturgical Consultation, the successor to the ecumenical ICET (International Consultation on English Texts). ELLC produced its first texts in *Praying Together* (Canterbury Press, 1988).

13   There was in 1992 a *legislative* exercise (which followed similar procedures to the liturgical business but was administered from the Legal Adviser's office) to revise the Canons relating to worship. This exercise made a number of significant adjustments to the Canons over and above the minor changes in the Canon on vesture, which attracted the most public attention. The Canon on experimental use of draft services was widened to make widespread and prolonged experimental use possible for the first time. More freedom was allowed in the arrangements for weekday Morning and Evening Prayer, encouraging people to gather for public prayer on weekdays 'as may best serve to sustain the corporate spiritual life of the parish and the pattern of life enjoined upon ministers by Canon C26.'

After well-received publication of *Patterns for Worship* (1995), the matter rested until the processes leading to *Common Worship* in 2000 were well advanced. It became clear in late 1997 that it would be necessary to amend *A Service of the Word* etc. to conform its texts to the emerging style for *Common Worship*. That process began with Deemed General Approval early in 1998 and a revision committee (chaired by Bishop Graham James of St Germans and including Trevor Lloyd, Brother Tristam SSF and Carole Cull from the Commission) decided to incorporate the ELLC texts of the Canticles though with minor changes to the Magnificat (GS 1280Y). After the revision stage in July, Final Approval was given in November 1998.

This revised form of *A Service of the Word* was designed to serve as a 'cover' for the forms of Morning and Evening Prayer which were in preparation (the Sunday forms were ready in time for the main publication of *Common Worship* in 2000; proposals for weekday Morning and Evening Prayer have subsequently appeared in the preliminary edition of *Daily Prayer*). This meant that there were no separate full Synod processes for the *Common Worship* forms of Morning and Evening Prayer. The intention in proceeding in this way was not to avoid Synod scrutiny of particular proposals, but to allow latitude in the precise forms of daily prayer to meet pastoral circumstances, while ensuring that they continued to be 'authorized alternatives' to the forms in the BCP, in conformity with Canon B11.

No separate publication of the revised form of *A Service of the Word* etc was issued in advance of *Common Worship* in 2000 but it was incorporated in a second edition of *Patterns* published (with revised layout and an expanded range of resources) in 2002 as *New Patterns for Worship* (Church House Publishing). The Commission of 1996–2001 set the work towards this revised edition in train at its final meeting in December 2000, mindful of the fact that the first edition was by then long out of print but continued much in demand. The new Commission oversaw the preparations from its first meeting in May 2001, appointing Trevor Lloyd to continue (as a Consultant) with the Commission for the duration of the work, having been the 'lead' member in this area from its first being proposed.

Calendar, Lectionary and Collects

The Promise of His Glory had been underpinned by an approach to Calendar (and consequently to Lectionary) in the autumn months which diverged from the ASB Calendar and Lectionary. The ASB had begun its annual cycle nine Sundays before Christmas with a sequence of Old Testament themes moving from Creation to John the Baptist and the Virgin Mary, the Sundays being described as 'before Christmas'. Those working on *The Promise of His Glory* were aware that in many places the middle parts of this sequence were eclipsed by Sunday observance of All Saints, by Remembrance Sunday and, in some places, by a borrowing of the Roman Catholic feast of Christ the King. If those 'November' themes were to be given any coherence in the proposed publication it would be awkward to maintain a parallel course with the eighth to fifth Sundays before Christmas. There was also perceived to be a strong resistance to the idea of 'beginning the church's year' in October.

There was also recurrent pressure throughout the period from 1980 for recognition to be given to the three–year Sunday eucharistic lectionary of the Roman church widely current in many provinces of the Anglican Communion and other denominations. This lectionary is organized on a completely different principle from the two–year Sunday eucharistic lectionary incorporated in ASB, with a framework based on continuous readings from week to week rather than a group of readings on a common theme. It would be uneasy for the two approaches to co–exist with equal status.

The catalyst for resumed consideration of these issues in the 1991–1996 Commission was the publication in the autumn of 1992 of a North American ecumenical reworking of the three year lectionary, *The Revised Common Lectionary*. An initial decision was also taken to develop work on calendar and lectionary in close collaboration with the other three Provinces in the British Isles: Scotland, Wales and Ireland, the 'Four Nations Group'.

The Commission was clear from March 1993 onwards that before any decision to move away from the ASB pattern was taken, underlying principles should be examined and widely discussed. What was the function of the public reading of scripture in worship? Should the passages be chosen sequentially or typologically? If a change were made from the thematic approach, were there alternative ways of highlighting certain central 'themes' in public liturgy which would be overlooked in a sequential reading of scripture? And, importantly, how could saints and heroes be selected and commemorated without disrupting the liturgy of the season?

It was also recognized that, given the English system of liturgical authorization, internationally recommended provisions (such as the Revised Common Lectionary) would inevitably be open to alteration in the Synod, causing irritation and misunderstanding. In July 1993 the Commission voted (a rare event) on eight questions posed by the sub–group. These votes recorded the Commission's commitment to a three–year Sunday eucharistic lectionary primarily based on the Revised Common Lectionary but also to the need to provide 'space' for particular churches to depart from this in favour of structured lectionary 'packages' (an idea 'floated' in *The Promise of His Glory*). There was also a marked reluctance to promote the anonymous 'weeks of Ordinary Time' or 'Proper 1, Proper 2, etc' and by September 1994 there was provisional agreement on 'after Trinity'.

The Sunday provision for second and third services (which is not from the *Revised Common Lectionary*) came from the drafting of consultants outside the Commission's membership. The development of the lectionary 'packages' (first put forward in *The Promise of His Glory*) has in more recent years resulted in the extensive provision in *New Patterns for Worship*.

By December 1994 this material and the work of the sub–group (inevitably bulky and detailed) came as one document to the Commission and went to the House of Bishops in January 1995. The Bishops' detailed comments were incorporated in a revised draft which went to Synod in July 1995 (GS 1161). The revision committee, formed from the new Synod which assembled in November 1995, was chaired by Bishop David Lunn of Sheffield, supported by four members of the Commission, Michael Perham, Brother Tristam SSF, Andrew Burnham and Jane Sinclair. The Revision Stage came in November 1996 and Final Approval in February 1997. *Calendar, Lectionary and Collects* came into authorized use from the First Sunday of Advent 1997. This had the effect of allowing the authorized use of the whole of the three–year Sunday lectionary in advance of *Common Worship*.

Inevitably in such a detailed provision inconsistencies came to light in use and many of these were remedied in a subsequent liturgical Synod procedure *Rules to Order the Service and Other Miscellaneous Liturgical Proposals* (GS 1342) which was introduced to the July 1999 Group of Sessions.

With regard to Collects the mandate to which the 'Four Nations' sub–group on *Calendar, Lectionary and Collects* worked was strongly influenced by a perceived need for Collects to reflect the content and register of the Prayer Book Collects. From autumn 1997 onwards work began on a traditional language version of the Collects to succeed the traditional language version of ASB Collects. Further work in Collect provision has continued since 2000 and, through a diocesan initiative in General Synod, an 'additional' series of (simplified) Collects has been authorized since February 2004.

The Office

The ASB Offices were closely modelled on the Prayer Book pattern. By the first meeting of the 1986–1991 Commission there was a feeling abroad that 'a fresh look at the Daily Office – including the distribution of psalmody and lectionary revision—seemed to be a widely felt need'.

An early discussion (after an article in *Theology* in January 1987 by one member, Bryan Spinks) set out the divergent approaches between those requiring a 'shape and structure for expressing regular and corporate prayer and praise' and the advocates of 'the ordered recitation of scripture and psalmody in course' as well as the need to provide material accessible to lay people who might usually follow Scripture Union and Bible Reading Fellowship patterns. In 1988 there was an Alcuin Club symposium and after that a group of members of the Commission and of the Society of St Francis worked together on revising its Office Book (published in 1992 in one form for use within the Franciscan community and another for general use—*Celebrating Common Prayer*). *Celebrating Common Prayer* incorporated some features from *The Promise of His Glory* (the opening 'Blessing of Light' and an alternative approach to weekday lectionary, particularly in the use of psalmody on a seasonal and day of the week basis). By the later stages of this work the 1991 Commission was formed and included Brother Tristam SSF. There were, however, no formal moves beyond monitoring various proposed forms of Daily Office (including, apart from *Celebrating Common Prayer*, *The Durham Office* and *Revised Daily Office* by the Joint Liturgical Group).

Another development arose as a spin–off from work in preparing the report *On the Way*: it was the concept of a 'knapsack' of basic prayers, scriptural passages and texts which faithful Christians might be encouraged to commit to memory for regular use. When *An Anglican Companion* eventually emerged from these proposals it also included a basic form of Daily Office, demonstrating the felt need for some 'official' framework for individuals structuring their daily pattern of prayer. Although these forms of Office had no legally authorized status, the sales of *Celebrating Common Prayer* indicated that the ASB Offices were not, for many, proving a satisfactory framework for daily prayer.

Although the forms now in *Daily Prayer* are heavily influenced by *Celebrating Common Prayer*, the Commission was aware that some found its structure too complex for convenient use, disliked its seasonal emphasis on different days of the week and the apportioning of psalms out of numerical order to times of day and season on a repeating pattern.

Serious work on the Daily Office began in 1997 and focussed at first on possible lectionary patterns which would complement those already authorized for use on Sundays. It was also known by then that the framework of *A Service of the Word* could be used for the Office. The Commission favoured this approach because it provided firm guidance on patterns of prayer *without* being proscriptive of other patterns which might continue in use and not be excluded from legitimate use. The sub–group dealing with this had, therefore, a dual remit from early 1997 (a) to work towards an authorized Weekday Lectionary, and (b) to develop patterns for daily prayer. An early decision was that, since *A Service of the Word* would certainly allow continued use of the ASB Offices, and it was proposed that *Common Worship* would include the Prayer Book Offices 'as used', there would be justification for *new* patterns, rather than modern language versions of BCP texts. The Commission also determined not to lose sight of the 1986 insight that it would be advantageous to link into the 'world' of Scripture Union and Bible Reading Fellowship.

Decisions had to be taken in time for the inclusion of the Sunday forms in the main volume of *Common Worship*. The tension between developed forms and a minimal structure suitable as a framework for daily prayer by individuals was resolved by the provision of a third form, 'Prayer During the Day'; approved forms for Night Prayer (Compline) are also included.

For the lectionary the shape of the new Calendar meant replacement of the ASB tables of office readings, and there were differing needs to be met. There were those wishing 'for a continuous reading of scripture in four or six"'tracks" as currently provided' but there were also 'many congregations with a different pattern of attendance where a sensible pattern of readings to meet episodic attendance was necessary'. There was also the difficult question of how far to abbreviate readings by 'filleting' (the process by which biblical narrative is compressed by omitting some verses within the passage).

The Commission looked at patterns elsewhere in the Anglican Communion and decided on two tracks of daily reading; one 'continuous' in the traditional manner, the other 'episodic'. The authorization process also included re–authorization of the Daily Eucharistic Lectionary[14] and that lectionary is available

---

14 The inclusion of this Roman Catholic provision in the ASB relatively unaltered was a decision of the late 1970s and there was general agreement that the provision should continue to be authorized. Enquiries suggested that there were no immediate plans for its revision by the Roman Catholic Church.

for use at the Daily Office if appropriate. The 'continuous' track of readings was taken from a North American pattern which had been adapted for use in Wales and the 'episodic' lectionary was newly commissioned work. The Synod processes were very close to the 2000 deadline and there was no opportunity to 'road test' the provision. For that reason it was given a limited life knowing that it would need to be revised in the light of use. In the event the present Commission has decided to replace the provision rather than revise it. The resulting weekday Lectionary has been before the Synod in 2004.

The Psalter

The issue of which version of the Psalter should be included in *Common Worship* proved to be a matter of some controversy and the published accounts of that are available in Synod papers (GS 1286, GS Misc 504, GS Misc 544 and GS Misc 582) and the record of Synod debates (in the *Report of Proceedings* for November 1997 and November 1999). That account is not repeated here, but some background reflections are offered.

The Psalter was of central importance in Church of England liturgy and piety from the sixteenth century onwards. The persistence of the Coverdale text, even after the general acceptance of the 1611 authorized version of the Bible, is well known, as is the popularity of succeeding metrical versions. It is well known that there was controversy up to the last moment as to which version of the Psalter should be included in the ASB, so it ought to have come as no great surprise that further controversy persisted in the preparations for *Common Worship*.

The Commission's view in preparing *Common Worship* was that authorization would inhere in the biblical references rather than in any particular 'authorized' translation. The wide variety of versions in current use (and the appearance of new versions) could not easily be regulated. The same was true of the Psalter and the authorization process was confined to the tables of lessons and psalmody. It was nevertheless necessary to include a Psalter in *Common Worship* for convenience in use. The evidence the Commission had towards the end of the 1980s was that by far the most frequently used Psalter continued to be Coverdale even in churches where the ASB was well established. 'Choirs and places where they sing' were well used to separate publications of the Coverdale Psalter with chant and the use of the psalms (apart from metrical versions in hymn books) was rapidly declining in frequency. The Commission's concern was to recover a central place for the Psalter and to make it easily available. The simple solution could well have been to continue the use of the ASB Psalter.[15]

There was evidence of a favourable reception of the American Psalter where *Celebrating Common Prayer* had been adopted but there were americanisms which might make it not wholly acceptable. By the mid 1990s the choice appeared to

---

15 A separate publication *The Collins Psalter*, for the English of which David Frost was responsible, had been adopted 'wholesale' for inclusion in the ASB (in preference to the *Revised Psalter* of the 1960s which was its rival in the 1979 debate).

lie between that and the ASB Psalter. One difficulty was the 'non–inclusive' nature of the language of the ASB Psalter.[16] There was also a strong (though not unanimous) view within the Commission that the liturgical use of the Psalter in Christian context was inevitably coloured by resonance in the tradition of its use (for example, the foreshadowings of the Passion in psalms 22 and 69) as well as the 'pure' translation from the Hebrew limited to the meaning of the text at the time it was written. That tension lay at the root of the public dispute which developed, though the Commission received synodical endorsement for its approach on three separate occasions. A draft of the proposed Psalter was also circulated for 'experimental use' and met with warmer reception than the ASB Psalter. Perhaps the more interesting issue still lies in the future; will the *Common Worship* Psalter be more successful in displacing Coverdale in general use than the ASB Psalter? And will it succeed in securing a more regular use of psalmody in worship in places where there are no choirs to lead Anglican chant?

---

16 An objection which was later overcome when Professor David Frost produced an inclusive version for use in *An Australian Prayer Book* in 1995.

5
From background to foreground: some issues

Prayer Book and Series One Issues

Prayer Book issues were before the Commission at all stages of discussing proposals for *Common Worship*. Most supporters of 'traditional language' seemed to be largely motivated by linguistic considerations, though there was always a number primarily concerned to safeguard the doctrinal position reflected in the wording of the mid–sixteenth century; this became a consideration later when the wording of Order Two was discussed in Synod revision committees. People were also concerned with the choice of versions of scripture, which lay beyond the Commission's remit but inevitably influenced the way in which alternative services were received locally.

There was a continuing demand for authorizing liturgies couched in Prayer Book language but not conforming precisely to the text printed in the 1662 Book. Such modifications, commonly referred to as 'Prayer Book as used', had been made for many years without controversy, but the publication of the *ASB* in 1980, excluding traditional language forms (apart from Rite B Holy Communion) highlighted the issue. From a viewpoint in Church House Westminster it appeared that local pastoral decisions were not always taken with sensitivity to those who wished to continue worshipping in Prayer Book language, though willing to accommodate variations from the order in 1662 (ranging from the 'interim rite' in anglo–catholic parishes to the omission of the penitential material before Morning and Evening Prayer and a wider variety of prayers 'after the third collect'). Before long there was shrill controversy and a well-organized and critical lobby in the Prayer Book Society. Some traditional language services continued to be authorized. Series Two Baptism and Confirmation, and Series One Marriage and Series One Funeral Services were renewed for five years in 1980 and 1985, but from 1990 authorization for Series Two Baptism and Confirmation lapsed. From 1990 Series One Marriage and Funeral Services have been renewed for five year periods[17] and have recently been authorized 'until further resolution of the Synod' (in effect, without time limit).

The minutes of the first meeting of the 1986 Commission concluded 'this continuing debate had been a consistent if dispiriting background to the work of the previous Commission and was now a nettle which needed to be grasped — more particularly to assist the House of Bishops out of a real and pressing difficulty'. The nature of this difficulty was that many bishops were being asked to sanction variations from the Prayer Book in traditional language which a strict interpretation of the Worship and Doctrine Measure 1974 would not allow. One of the tasks undertaken by the 1981–1986 Commission had been to produce

---

17 In March 1990 however, the House of Laity denied a further authorization to Series One Funerals, causing the House of Bishops to engineer a re–introduction of the proposal in July 1990 when these services did secure further authorization.

traditional language versions of the ASB Collects, which could be allowed by the 'minor variation' permission in Canon B5.

The Commission considered various options—the issuing of guidance by the bishops as to how far 'discretion' might go, synodical amendment of the rubrics of the Book of Common Prayer, and further attempts to re–authorize Series One. After discussion with Legal Officers and the House of Bishops, the decision was taken to introduce proposals for amendments to Rite B to Synod in February 1987, using a shortened procedure on the basis that the proposals were uncontentious. This was not accepted by the Standing Committee of the General Synod, which thought the full procedure ought to be followed. In the light of that decision the proposals for adaptation of Rite B did not go forward. At the same time John Bickersteth, Bishop of Bath and Wells, had proposed a motion to the General Synod that the traditional language version of the Lord's Prayer should be substituted for the modified ICET version printed in ASB. The Commission sponsored an amendment providing for choice between the modified traditional and modern language versions whenever the text of the Lord's Prayer appeared (except in Rite B when it would continue to be used in the modified traditional version only). The amendment was passed and reflected in subsequent printings of the ASB.

In the wake of these developments the House of Bishops (advised by the Commission) decided that individual bishops would so interpret their duties under Canon B5 (minor variations in public worship) as to treat any form of service which at any time had enjoyed authorized status (thus including Series One and Series Two services in traditional language) as if they were 'minor variations'. This decision gave rise to criticism, but after initial flurry the immediate pressure seemed to recede as far as the bishops were concerned. Insensitive and controversial decisions at parish level undoubtedly continued, as did shrill protests from the Prayer Book Society.

The 1986–1991 Commission's 'end of term report' *The Worship of the Church as it approaches the Third Millennium* (GS Misc 364) recognized that there was need to continue to work at 'the relationship of future liturgical work to the continuing Prayer Book tradition'. The Commission wished it to be clear that 'although no conclusion or solutions had yet emerged it had, throughout its work, been concerned to work towards a synthesis which was not 'confrontational'.

The Commission tackled these underlying issues about Anglican identity and diversity and the nature of liturgical language in the essays published in *The Renewal of Common Prayer* (GSMisc 412, CHP 1993) and also in response to a submission from the Prayer Book Society.

By then the Commission's membership included Baroness James, a Vice President of the Prayer Book Society *(alias* P.D.James, the author). Both the Society and the Commission valued opportunities to engage in conversation, and one result was the publication of *Model and Inspiration* (SPCK 1993), which comprised the Prayer Book Society's submission, the Commission's response and the papers delivered at a *Praxis* symposium in November 1992. The following year there was debate on these issues in the House of Lords, for which Baroness James' good offices were a valuable resource. While tensions remained and the Society and Commission agendas continued to diverge, there was now a channel for communication. The Commission, for its part, was confirmed in its provisional view that the revision of the eucharistic rites in ASB would need if possible, to provide a common rite presented in two language registers.

Inclusive Language

It is now commonplace to observe that the *ASB* was published before questions of 'gender inclusive' language came to general awareness. The *Lent, Holy Week, Easter* compilation of the 1981-1986 Commission began to engage with the principle of gender inclusiveness. In March 1986 the newly appointed Commission saw that it would need to address the principles involved and build them into its future work. *Ad hoc* 'gender inclusive' adaptation of existing texts was beginning and would continue apace. The Commission, however, determined to work from first principles. It noted in 1986 that 'concerns over gender specific language had equal implication for racial or hierarchically distinctive terms. In seeking to serve truth by redressing the imbalance of such expressions, more important truths regarding human perception of the Divine might be obscured.'

A report on the issues entitled *Making Women Visible* (GS 859) was presented to the House of Bishops in October 1988 and debated in Synod in July 1989. Sixteen years later, the problematic ASB phrases which it sought to modify are themselves largely superseded, but the principles set out in the introductory essay remain as the Commission's guiding principles in this area.

The seriousness with which the Commission has taken language is illustrated by the extended engagement with the issues at the inaugural meeting of the 1996–2001 Commission with Professor Valentine Cunningham. Two underlying watchwords emerged:

(a) the need to consider carefully in each context the proper distinction between three 'voices', the leader of worship, the worshippers as a congregational body and the personal address to the needs of individuals; and

(b) the fruitful possibilities which might ensue from attention to metonymy as well as metaphor.

These principles were brought to bear on the emerging texts for *Common Worship* in a further report *Language and the Worship of the Church* (GS 1115) debated in General Synod in July 1994. By that time the need was no longer guidance on adapting existing texts, rather criteria to be followed in new drafting; continuing use of traditional language texts; the case for adopting the most recent round of internationally and ecumenically agreed texts produced by ELLC and the choice of biblical and psalter translations to accompany and underpin liturgical drafting. At every stage, sensitive and subtle doctrinal nuance and theological considerations were raised as well as the earlier strand of avoiding gender specific words.

The Commission set its face firmly against tampering with the 'given' of historic texts (such as those from the 1662 Prayer Book). Some texts reflect the understanding of their own time and cannot be wrenched into an early twenty–first century mode without aesthetic, doctrinal and semantic violence being done to them. New texts, however, must rightly be composed and then judged by current criteria and expectations.

Doctrinal Considerations

Issues of language (both traditional and inclusive) bring doctrinal issues into sharp focus. An awareness of the centrality of doctrinal considerations in its work has characterized all the Commission's discussions.

The Commission's Constitution urges cross–reference to the Doctrine Commission, if possible by common membership. This has proved consistently difficult to achieve. On the other hand, membership of the Commission has always included scholarly seriousness and, as has been pointed out in at least two reports to General Synod, the theological credentials of its members have at periods equalled those of members of the Doctrine Commission. It has never been far from the Commission's consciousness that our Church's doctrine is to be found in authorized liturgy, and that enquirers and ecumenical dialogues are directed to the liturgical texts. Membership of the Commission has consistently included one person with working expertise in biblical studies and there have been occasions when discursive discussion has been called to order by serious attention to the Greek or Hebrew text.

The particular relationship between the Commission and the House of Bishops, frequently involving the House's Theological Group, safeguards that doctrinal seriousness. It is inevitable, however, that some bishops, pressured by many concerns, may not bring detailed theological scrutiny to the texts brought to them; it is thus the more important that the Commission exercises serious attention on its own behalf. Doctrinal issues that have given rise to prolonged discussion include prayer and the departed, the provision of funeral services for the stillborn, the anamnesis and epiclesis in eucharistic prayer, doctrinal implications of practices which spring up in the context of ecumenical worship and the theological underpinning to disparate work on Initiation, Wholeness and Healing, and Reconciliation.

From time to time the Commission has sought opportunity to draw more public attention to these issues and to seek wider participation in discussions before the particularities of liturgical text are addressed. Examples of this are the provision of a statement of the theological rationale for funeral services for a child dying near the time of birth, the two symposia of General Synod members on issues of Prayer and the Departed in July 1995 and July 1996 before funeral service texts were presented; the presentation on eucharistic prayer at the General Synod in July 1997 and theological contributions to such publications as *The Renewal of Common Prayer.*

An important element has been the participation of members of the Commission in the International Anglican Liturgical Consultations (IALC) from which have come Anglican statements on Children and Communion,

Inculturation in liturgy, Initiation, the Eucharist and Orders. Such international statements provide both a yardstick by which the Church of England's liturgical provision in these areas must be measured, and a corrective to insular attitudes.

The Lord's Prayer

The text of the Lord's Prayer to be used in public worship has been the subject of heated discussion from the 1970s. Agreement in the (British) Joint Liturgical Group (JLG) in the 1960s secured the use of the 'Modified Traditional' text of the Lord's Prayer in common between the Church of England Series 2 services, the early translation into English of the Roman rite and in a number of other denominations. It went no further than such minor changes as 'who art' instead of 'which art'. In the 1970s two reports of the International Consultation on English Texts (ICET) proposed modern English translations which were adopted into the liturgies of various churches including Series 3 Holy Communion for the Church of England (it is of significance for subsequent debates that this modern English translation was never adopted by the Roman Catholic church). Controversy, for the Church of England, centred on the line which was rendered in Series Three (not exactly as recommended by ICET) as 'do not bring us to the time of trial'. At the revision of Series 3 Holy Communion (Rite A in the ASB) the ICET 'Save us from the time of trial' was recommended by the Commission and the revision committee, but it was attacked in Synod, and 'Lead us not into temptation' was restored. The ELLC translations which appeared in 1988 retained 'Save us from the time of trial' and it was the Commission's starting position that such an ecumenically and internationally agreed text ought to be proposed for the next round of liturgical revision in the Church of England. The issues were fully set out in the Commission's report *Language and the Worship of the Church* (GS 1115) debated in July 1994, which revealed that there remained strong resistance to any move away from 'Lead us not into temptation'.

Because of that, and the strength of feeling over the Bishop of Bath and Wells' proposal in 1987[18] to drop any modern English translation, it was judged politic to deal with the Lord's Prayer in a separate piece of liturgical business on the understanding that whatever was agreed would be 'slotted in' to each service.

The Liturgical Commission report (GS 1271) to the Synod in February 1998 provided ELLC's rationale for its proposed text, together with information about the then current ecumenical situation.

The central importance of this issue was signalled by the Chairmanship of the Revision Committee being taken by the Archbishop of York; the Commission was represented by David Stancliffe, Carole Cull and Michael Perham. The reports of the Committee's work (GS 1271Y and GS 1271X) were finely balanced between continuing the ASB modern translation or changing to the ELLC translation. The second revision stage came down in favour of continuing the ASB translation (alongside the continued availability of the modified traditional) but with two significant 'glosses'. Synod decided that the ELLC translation ('save

18 See above, p 21.

us from the time of trial') should appear somewhere in the corpus of revised liturgy in 2000 as available for use on 'appropriate occasions', though not included in the text of any particular rite. It also decided that on all occasions where the text of the Lord's Prayer was printed in a service it should appear in both forms (even in traditional language rites), the only differentiation being that the text printed first should be that in the register of the service as a whole so that, for the most part, the modern English version is printed first but in traditional language services the Modified Traditional version comes first. Thus on page 106 of *Common Worship* the text of the Lord's Prayer for use on suitable occasions is printed with the line 'Save us from the time of trial' and in Holy Communion Order One in Traditional Language (page 222 of *Common Worship*) the modern English translation is included as well as the Modified Traditional. But in Morning and Evening Prayer from the Book of Common Prayer, and Order Two Holy Communion (which adheres closely to the Book of Common Prayer), the view was taken that the unmodified traditional version ('which art') should be used.

6
From Cradle to Grave

Initiation

Since 1980 the Liturgical Commission has devoted considerable time to underlying Initiation themes before detailed drafting of services for baptism, confirmation, renewal of commitment, wholeness and healing, reconciliation, nurture in the faith and catechesis.

The 1986–1991 Commission discussions were largely reactive to outside requests for advice. These included pressures felt in the House of Bishops to provide a rite of recommitment to the Christian faith to counter growing pressures in some contexts for 'rebaptism', work on a revision of the Catechism (largely done by the Board of Education), and an increasing awareness through a number of Board of Education reports (eg *Children in the Way* (GS 1988)) of the need to provide liturgical elements in Christian nurture. A link between the call for reaffirmation of Christian commitment and reconciliation of a penitent was reflected in the Commission's advice to the House of Bishops in *The Initiation Conundrum* (GS Misc 366) prepared at the end of 1989 and contributing to the House of Bishops mounting a full Synod debate on initiation in July 1991.

The motions passed by General Synod in 1991 came prior to the agreement of the IALC Toronto statement (*Christian Initiation in the Anglican Communion*, Grove Worship Series 118); the context was set for five years of work within the Commission on such matters as the revision of the initiation services in ASB, input into any rite for 'renewing' baptism, work on catechism, nurture in the faith and catechumenate rites, admission of children to communion before confirmation (not at that stage ratified in Synod), and further work in the area of reconciliation.

One immediate result of the 1991 debate was the establishment of a working party of members of the Board of Education, the Board of Mission and the Liturgical Commission to produce a document on Christian nurture. This work proceeded independently of the Commission's meetings (though with large input from the Commission's representatives in the group (David Stancliffe and Michael Vasey)). It was eventually published in 1995 as *On the Way* (GS Misc 444).

The Commission recognized that to most church people a connection between baptism, reconciliation and healing as well as use of the 'package' word 'Initiation' might not be obvious. There would need to be carefully argued explanation of the connections, rooted in biblical reference. A sub–group established in the autumn of 1991 met throughout the quinquennium, reporting progress to the full Commission. So the meetings of the Commission in March and June 1993, and March and September 1994 were each punctuated by three or four separate discussions of initiation drafts. These drafts were seen by the House of Bishops in June and October 1994 and again in January 1995 when the bulk of an eight-part report was approved for transmission to Synod. Considerable unease was expressed in the House of Bishops about the part of the report dealing with reconciliation (the memory of the defeat of Reconciliation of a Penitent in 1983 remained fresh), and from October 1994 work in that area came to a halt until after 2000.

After revision in the light of House of Bishops' discussions (and omitting the section on Reconciliation), the report was circulated to the last meeting of the outgoing Synod in July 1995 (GS 1152). The revision committee was chaired by Bishop John Hind (of Gibraltar in Europe) and included David Stancliffe, Michael Vasey (until his death in 1998) and Robert Willis (replaced after he left the Commission by Anna de Lange).

The revision committee took an immediate decision to divide its work into two parts, deferring work on *Wholeness and Healing* until Synod authorized Baptism, Confirmation, Reaffirmation and Reception. This meant that, since the same revision committee dealt with the business throughout (a total of seven stages in Synod) its work was not completed until February 2000. It could never be argued that Initiation issues did not receive a thorough scrutiny, first in the Commission and second in that General Synod revision committee.

The revision committee produced four reports (GS 1152Y, X, V and W) which detail the issues which came under discussion. Once Synod had given Final Approval to the first part of the work (Baptism, Confirmation, Reaffirmation and Reception) those rites were authorized for liturgical use from Easter 1998. In the final stages of preparation for *Common Worship* some rubrical modifications of the Baptism rite were authorized to meet the complaint that in the light of experience the rite was too long for use in the context of a main act of Sunday worship—largely because the cumulative effect of the revision committee's work had been to increase the mandatory as opposed to optional elements in the baptism service. This reflects common experience that the process of revision invariably lengthens texts which were intended to be brief.

The postponement of consideration of rites for Wholeness and Healing until a later stage of the revision committee's work meant that the committee had to wrestle with accommodating the insights of the report *A Time to Heal*, (CHP 2000) which was not even commissioned when the liturgical drafts were first introduced to Synod in July 1995. Also in the second stage of its work the revision committee added to the proposed rites for Wholeness and Healing the proposals for revision of *Ministry to the Sick*.

After publication of *On the Way*, the likelihood that the House of Bishops would issue guidelines for admitting children to communion before confirmation clarified the scope for the Commission's further work on rites for stages in a catechumenate. Some preliminary drafts were published in the summer of 1998 (*Rites on the Way*, GS Misc 530), largely compiled and written by Michael Vasey. His untimely death within weeks of publication meant that there was little subsequent opportunity to resume work in this area. The missing elements are now being added.[19]

Once work on initiation services entered the Synod revision processes, the Commission itself seldom returned to these matters but there was agreement

19 Synod debate in July 2004 and Commendation expected in 2005.

that further public debate on reconciliation would best be prepared for by general discussion of the underlying issues, stimulated by a book of essays, for which an outline was produced in 1994, Time and energy did not allow such a publication to emerge before the matter came to Synod in 2004. A definitive publication of *Common Worship: Initiation Services* will now follow.

When the authorized initiation services were published in 1998, a commentary by the Liturgical Commission was included, restating the key elements from the Commission's original report to General Synod (GS 1152, July 1995). It has been a characteristic of Church of England liturgical publications that, without such commentary, the explanatory introductions from the Commission to General Synod, when drafts are first introduced for debate, and the subsequent explanation of changes made by revision committees in their reports are seldom available to the wider Church. Partly in recognition of this the Commission has, in the course of the 1990s pressed for the inclusion of 'pastoral introductions' as *part of* the authorized rites, and in *A Service of the Word* included a substantial commentary as an integral part of the order.

Funerals

The 1986–1991 Commission worked on two refinements of the ASB provision which appeared as Commended rites. First, responding to growing pastoral concern since the mid–1970s when the ASB funeral services were drawn up, came the provision of a funeral for stillborn children, which the Commission broadened to include a child 'dying near the time of birth'. While there was much pastoral sympathy for this, any public recognition for such services had to engage with the theological issue of whether a Christian funeral service is appropriate for a foetus which did not come to live birth. The Commission sought advice from the Regius Professor of Moral Theology at Oxford, Oliver O'Donovan, and a note based on his advice was published as the preface to the commended rite when it appeared. The rite continues to be available in *Common Worship* with the theological comment still attached (*Common Worship: Pastoral Services* page 316). The provision is largely a compilation from the resources available for the funeral of a child with suitable additional material. A delegation of hospital chaplains visiting the Commission in May 1990 made representations that this provision was still too formal but the Commission's position was that there are freedoms which cannot be signalled in an official liturgical publication which might nevertheless be taken by a pastor in the circumstances of individual tragedy.

The second matter related to a stage before the funeral, Ministry at the Time of Death. Correspondence in 1987 questioned the 'tone' of the provision for anointing in *Ministry to the Sick*. The expectation in *Ministry to the Sick* was, clearly, physical recovery; the correspondent was chaplain in a hospice where the invariable expectation was that the patient was shortly to die. The Commission decided to involve him in the initial drafting, as a means of ensuring that the provision was appropriate.

There was at that date, (before women were priested and yet women deacons were hospital chaplains), discussion about whether anointing should invariably be administered by a priest. The Commission decided to use the term 'minister' throughout and to explain in the notes the tradition of the minister of anointing being bishop or priest. The 1990 publication made reference to diaconal anointing when the bishop allowed, but this is not continued in Common Worship, which refers to Canon Law which restricts anointing to bishops and priests.

In 1992 the 1991–96 Commission noted that the funeral services 'were amongst the more frequently criticized of those in ASB and most in need of revision'. A 'brainstorming' discussion in March 1993 highlighted six concerns:

(a) the need for a collection of rites focussed on different moments in the process of dying

(b) the need to take seriously the limitation of twenty minutes at 'the crem'.

(c) 'growing desire for tangible symbols and actions, something "to do".'

(d) 'growing reality that many "church" funerals . . . would be for the unbaptized'.

(e) the funeral recognized to be a point of pastoral contact for proclaiming the faith, 'but *how* to proclaim Christ in such a context'?

(f) all the issues surrounding prayer and the departed.

After further substantial discussion in July 1993 expressions of view from the general public were invited via the church press. The sub–group for this matter brought material to the Commission in February 1995: one result was the decision to hold a symposium on *Prayer and the Departed* at the July 1995 General Synod. This became a two–year process, a second symposium being held in July 1996. Consultation with a wide spectrum of opinion at an early stage was vital to securing agreement. At the Commission's first sight of proposals from its sub–group there was unease at the suggested way of dealing with symbols of the deceased's life, the extended nature of the entry rites and provision for two addresses. By the time the 1991–96 Commission went out of office, the major work on the funeral service was complete. The new Commission took the view that nothing should go forward which would not be acceptable to all members of the Commission; but drafts could go to the House of Bishops by January 1997.

The Bishops' reception of the drafts was positive, and they agreed in June 1997 that the draft rites should be distributed for experimental use in authorized parishes. By January 1998 responses from the parishes were seen on the whole to be favourable. Some questioned whether the material could be accommodated within the standard 'twenty minute slot'. Others questioned whether the funeral service was 'too Christian'! The Commission was encouraged to take the work forward to the June 1998 House of Bishops and the General Synod in July 1998.

By that time it was combined with proposals for Marriage and Thanksgiving for the Birth of a Child, and introduced to the Synod under the general title of *Pastoral Rites*. The revision committee was chaired by David Bentley, Bishop of Gloucester, and the Commission members were Trevor Lloyd, Andrew Burnham and Anna de Lange. Despite the committee's fear of possible criticisms in Synod, there was no remission to a second revision committee stage for the funeral rites and (after Marriage had 'caught up') Final Approval was given in February 2000. It may perhaps be claimed that the case for thorough preparation and widespread prior discussion was proved.

Marriage

After the debates on the Marriage Commission report of 1978 it was clear that the Commission would not be asked to 'adapt' the marriage service for use after divorce, but the House of Bishops asked for help in bringing some order into the widespread practice of services of 'blessing' after civil marriage. The Commission devised a common form from the various forms of prayer used in separate dioceses. This was shown to the Bishops and to Synod in June/July 1984 (in the context of debates about marriage of the divorced). Although the primary context was the pastoral need to minister to those who had a civil marriage after divorce, it was recognized that there were other circumstances in which a Register Office marriage might be followed by forms of prayer and no reference to divorce was included in the title or Notes. Because of strongly–expressed reservations in General Synod the word 'blessing' was scrupulously avoided, hence the title *Prayer and Dedication*.

The House of Bishops duly commended these forms of prayer which were published in Autumn 1985 and have continued in widespread use ever since. Although *Common Worship* includes forms of prayer and thanksgiving for a marriage (primarily intended to be used on significant anniversaries or after a period of estrangement) the form of prayer after civil marriage continued to meet a need and was included in *Common Worship: Pastoral Services*.

Before the Commission returned to marriage as a substantive issue in October 1996 it had concurred in proposals to extend authorization to the Series One Marriage rite at the end of each quinquennium, commented in 1989 on early proposals for the revision of the Roman Catholic marriage rite and had notice of the Joint Liturgical Group proposals for an 'ecumenical' marriage rite in 1993.

The same sub–group of Commission members working on funerals turned its attention to Marriage at the beginning of the 1996–2001 quinquennium, with the remit that as there was general satisfaction with the ASB rite it should not be unduly altered.

At its first meeting the 1996–2001 Commission explored the possibilities of enlarging the theological frame of reference in the ASB rite to include a more 'Eastern' sense of marriage as 'gift from God' to counter the prevailing rationale of 'contract', and extending the rite by forms of prayer to mark stages in the process from engagement to celebration of significant anniversaries.[20]

Initial discussion in the House of Bishops raised again the question of whether special forms should be available for marriage after a divorce. The Commission

---

20 'Political' considerations saw to it at an early stage that liturgical celebration of engagement was abandoned; the risks of such a rite being taken as signalling church approval for cohabitation set too many alarm bells ringing in episcopal and wider circles.

took the view 'that the appropriate way forward once the parties came to the point of marriage would be for the normal marriage rite to be used' with no suggestion of a 'second class' status. The possibility of authorizing some of the JLG rite to enable more significant participation by ministers of other denominations in what would remain legally a Church of England service was considered in 1997.

After these initial discussions a draft was circulated to those parishes authorized to experiment by the beginning of the autumn of 1997, unfortunately just as the 'wedding season' came to an end: but the inexorable synodical timetable leading to 2000 could not have allowed a longer period. At the request of the House of Bishops the 'mainstream' text retained ASB wording but with the Commission's suggested alternative introduction in an appendix. Experimental use was valuable for instance in showing that the Commission's alternative would command more support than the ASB form, and the two introductions were reversed in the Synod revision committee.

The texts were introduced to General Synod in July 1998 as part of the 'Pastoral Rites' package, with Funerals and Thanksgiving for the Birth of a Child. The work of the revision committee was reported in GS 1298Y. Although before the Synod process controversy had been expected to centre on the funeral services, it was the marriage service which was remitted to a second revision committee stage in July 1999 on the narrow issue of forsaking 'all other' or 'all others'. No change was made and Final Approval was given in February 2000.

Despite doubts in the Commission (because of its lack of flexibility), and some discussion of the possibility of a traditional language version of the *Common Worship* marriage rite, the Series One marriage rite was renewed for a further five years.[21] (It has subsequently been further renewed without specified time limit.)

It is worthwhile reflecting that what began as a very strongly–expressed wish to retain the ASB rite virtually unaltered nonetheless led to a widening of the scope of the theological resonances and frame of reference, not least in the variety of prayers and forms of nuptial blessing available for optional use. It is also worth noting that the Synod was prepared to give *carte blanche* authorization to the pre–existing JLG marriage rite as an option to be used as a 'rite of the established church' when allowed by the Ordinary.

Thanksgiving for the Gift of a Child

The ASB included *Thanksgiving for the Birth of a Child* and *Thanksgiving after Adoption*, both seen as alternatives to the BCP's *Churching of Women,* so revision of the ASB rites would be expected to require full synodical procedure. In the Commission's thinking, however, this was but one of a series of pastoral rites surrounding birth and entry into the Christian faith which could largely be

---

21   It is more than likely (whatever the letter of the law) that the freedoms available in the *Common Worship* rite are increasingly taken in the second part of the Series One service.

provided by the 'commended' route, and were outlined in *Rites on the Way* (GS Misc 530).

However, *Thanksgiving for the Birth of a Child* became more prominent than the other rites both because of the synodical process and also because of continuing debate in the Church (focussed in the Synod debates on Christian initiation in July 1991) whether thanksgiving could be perceived as an alternative to baptism for the 'less committed'. From the Commission's point of view, the *Thanksgiving for the Gift of a Child* (deliberately worded to cover both birth and adoption) was always seen as a separate pastoral rite, quite distinct from baptism. In the Commission's discussions between December 1997 and April 1998 the need for nuance in the distinction between thanksgiving and baptism led to careful attention to the detail of the proposals, and also to the decision to include the rite in the 'Pastoral Rites' package. This was largely a matter of timing and use of resources, but also because a separate process might have seemed to signal a substantive 'alternative' to baptism. The course of that Synod and revision committee discussion is to be found in the relevant sections of GS 1298Y and the Report of Proceedings

7
Eucharist and Ministry

Eucharistic Prayers

After the first Synod debate on *Patterns for Worship*, with its range of new eucharistic prayers (February 1990), future work on eucharistic revision stood remitted to the House of Bishops under the heading 'Rite C'. The commendation of *Patterns for Worship* and the authorization of *A Service of the Word* meant that from the mid–1990s there was considerable freedom to adapt the first part of the eucharist, utilizing the provision for combining a Service of the Word with Holy Communion. The way in which these matters developed conspired to separate the revision of eucharistic prayers and the revision of the eucharistic rites as a whole into two separate processes. This was reflected in the work of the Commission itself and subsequently in Synod.

Concern on the part of the 1986–1991 Commission over the wording of eucharistic prayers had its antecedents. Reaching agreement entails the reconciliation of two aims. On the one hand the text of the 'Prayer of Consecration' is acknowledged by all to have doctrinal and theological weight. Whatever texts are authorized in General Synod have significance for Anglican eucharistic theology. On the other hand, carefully crafted doctrinal nuance in a presidentially spoken text is judged to be a pastoral handicap in assemblies which are increasingly unaware of historical and theological context, particularly when significant numbers of children/young people are present.

For the Church of England it had been groundbreaking in the mid–1960s for the familiar phrases of the Prayer Book to be supplemented by the Series 2 prayers. By 1986 it was recent history that these had been augmented by a 'Hippolytan' text, introduced during the course of the Synod revision process in 1978 (ASB Rite A, Third Eucharistic Prayer). That same revision process had also dealt with requests for 'special' prayers for use, eg with the sick or with children. The result had been the inclusion of the Rite A First Eucharistic Prayer 'abbreviated' for use with the sick, but the rejection of special prayers for use when children were present. Requests for a children's prayer continued, augmented after *Faith in the City* by requests for simple and short eucharistic prayers for UPA situations. The ASB prayer for use with the sick was, in practice, being used in mainstream Sunday services.

Against that background, it was recognized that any work on a 'directory' for a freer approach to liturgy in UPA, 'family' service, and children's contexts would have to engage with the question of the eucharistic prayer.

In March 1987 the Commission were told 'The demands for alternatives were becoming so strident that it had to be recognized that if texts commended by the Commission were not authorized for experimental use, unsanctioned experiment with unauthorized texts would undoubtedly occur'. The minute states that 'there would be some who would make use of texts which were intended only for discussion' and that experimental use could not 'patronizingly, be limited to designated UPAs'. At that stage discussion centred on three texts, based on (a) a text put forward for discussion in the Roman Catholic journal *Liturgy* by Fr Alan Griffith; (b) an early version of an ICEL Eucharistic Prayer which was a precursor of the Roman Catholic fourth Eucharistic Prayer; and (c) a responsive form produced by the sub–group. Some saw ambiguous phrases capable of resonating differing meanings as a valuable element of mystery and openness, whilst others were concerned that in this context there would be pressure in Synod for clarity. The responsive text under discussion even canvassed the possibility of omitting an institution narrative but it was admitted that there would be 'unease at so marked a departure from custom'. It was also recognized that it would be impossible to limit alternative eucharistic prayers to particular and special occasions alongside more normative use of 'standard' prayers.

The Commission was concerned throughout the ensuing exercise for 'some basic popular teaching on the form, function and rationale of the Eucharistic Prayer within the rite as a whole'; one result was the presentation to General Synod on 'Eucharistic Prayer' (July 1997, published as *Eucharistic Prayer in the Church of England*, GS Misc 512).

A fourth text was introduced from September 1988, partly in response to reinforced requests for extreme brevity in eucharistic prayer (heard in a series of visits to UPAs that year). As the time for discussing texts with the House of Bishops approached, another practical concern was the anticipated pressure for one unvarying text of the narrative of institution in every eucharistic prayer, conflicting with the 'unbalancing' effect of such a text on prayers drafted with brevity in mind.

Nearly all the doctrinal and pastoral tensions thrown up by proposed texts for eucharistic prayer were present within the Commission's internal discussions in the second half of the 1980s, and to some extent those tensions surfaced in the Synod debate in February 1990. On the whole, however, the Commission was persuaded that it was right to keep as many options in the forum of discussion to as late a stage in the processes as possible, recognizing that an innate conservatism about this central part of the rite might easily foreclose discussion of more radical options and thus do nothing to diminish the clamour of those calling for shorter and more participatory prayers.

The Commission returned to the subject in May 1992. The House of Bishops had asked the Commission to note recent ecumenical work on eucharistic prayers, possibly taking the anaphora of St Basil as a basis. There were

> 'two possible meanings attached to "ecumenical" in this context. First, a text such as that of Basil coming from an era before the main schisms of Christian history had the potential to form the basis for a prayer which would be accepted across denominational boundaries. Second, there could be ecumenical agreement on the use of existing prayers from other denominations and parts of the world. A distinct advantage of the first

approach was its potential in Local Ecumenical Projects and other such situations of ecumenical co–operation, in providing an agreed basis from which to work on homespun liturgical texts rather than the *ab initio* drafting which often took place'.

'One problem with using the Prayer of St Basil as a basis was its length'. 'Other difficulties which would need to be faced in honest theological discussion within the Anglican context were the wording of the Epiclesis on both gifts and people, positioned as it was in prayers based on Basil, after the institution narrative'.

This work on an ecumenically based eucharistic prayer had to be related to continuing revision of the four texts ('Rite C') in *Patterns for Worship* and the demands in Synod for prayers (plural) 'for use when children are present'. In that latter context further discussion took the (then) recently–issued Roman Catholic prayers for use with children as a base. The initial reaction was that any such drafts would need to be the subject of wide consultation and trial use before firm proposals were taken to the House of Bishops.

The potential timetable was longer than that envisaged by those clamouring for urgent action, but the Commission resolved to prepare the ground thoroughly before bringing proposals into the public domain. As part of its work there was commissioned in May 1992 (from a unit in the Diocese of Southwell) a series of video presentations using the draft texts in a context where children were present in different situations and styles of worship. The Commission went to the House of Bishops in January 1994 with five prayers, reflecting all four of the 1989 *Patterns* texts with one additional children's text. It was seen as 'essential to accompany the text of any prayer for use when children were present with notes emphasising the need for careful attention to be paid to the way in which the prayer was presented for children to appreciate the central importance of the prayer in the whole rite.'

The mood in the House of Bishops was cautious about taking forward any proposals for additional eucharistic prayers, though (as the Commission noted with a 'measure of frustration')

'the collective caution of the House of Bishops ... did not reflect the common and widespread toleration by individual Bishops of relatively uncontrolled use of unauthorized texts in diverse local contexts. If in their own Dioceses bishops recognised the strong pastoral factors calling for such provision, why had they not been able to allow proposals to go forward into the properly–constituted channels for revision and authorization?'

The House of Bishops had elected to take matters out of the Commission's hands and to present a report to the July 1994 General Synod in its own name (which incidentally allowed members of the Commission to speak more freely in the debate) on the basis of a report (GS 1120) which presented all five of the Commission's texts for comment, but reserved to the House itself decisions on which, if any, of the texts to put into the synodical procedure.

For the Commission one consequence of this decision was to prolong the process of bringing any additional eucharistic prayers into authorized use, thus minimizing the experience to be gained before it would be necessary to revise the ASB prayers. Fortunately, revision of the Canons on liturgy had recently extended the possibilities for experimental use of liturgical material and the Commission decided (September 1994) that it would use that provision for draft eucharistic prayers so as to maximize feedback. The Commission also resolved to start on its own proposals for revising the ASB Eucharistic rites, since that would necessarily include some revisiting of the texts of the four eucharistic prayers in Rite A (and the two variants in traditional language in Rite B) and it would need to relate that revision to the texts of any additional eucharistic prayers eventually authorized.

One feature of the General Synod debate in July 1994 was an evident expression of dissatisfaction about the adequacy of the drafts for use where many children were present. In the event, the House of Bishops (at its October 1994 meeting) decided to return two only of the Commission's five draft prayers for the synodical procedure, but also to commission a new draft from the Commission, working jointly with the Board of Education. At General Synod in November 1994 General Approval was given to the two prayers put forward (GS 1138) and a revision committee chaired by Archdeacon Timothy Raphael began work in December 1994, leading to the Revision Stage in July 1995. Three members of the Commission (Trevor Lloyd, Bishop Pat Harris of Southwell and Mark Dalby) served on the committee. At the same time, a joint group from the Commission and the Board of Education worked at the requested draft which came to the revision committee and then on to the Synod in July 1995. That committee, in response to submissions made to it from members of Synod, restored two of the original package of five prayers in GS 1120 and, in addition, included a responsive form of the first Eucharistic Prayer from Rite A (importing an element of congregational participation into an already established 'mainstream' eucharistic prayer). Thus in total six prayers came back to the Synod from the revision committee when only two (with the long–term promise of a third) had been remitted to it. This appeared to be in accord with the mind of Synod, as no motions to refer the prayers back to the revision committee were even tabled, let alone approved. The drafts thus stood remitted to the House of Bishops, prior to Final Approval in General Synod.

Since the House was not meeting until October 1995 time constraints made it impossible for the Synod to consider Final Approval in November (which was, in any case, the first meeting of a newly elected General Synod). In January 1996 the House agreed that the matter should come to General Synod in February 1996. There it failed to gain two–thirds majority in the House of Laity. Thus the proposals fell.

There were complex reasons and a combination of factors (not least the need for a newly elected Synod which had had no part in the drafting or approval of the texts to give two–thirds majority approval to them) for the failure of these additional eucharistic prayers. The House of Bishops was shown to have underestimated the pressures for wide variety in eucharistic prayer (though its caution undoubtedly represented one section of church opinion). Others felt that the proposals were not radical enough to meet pressing pastoral situations.[21]

At its final meeting the 1991–96 Commission reflected that 'the failure to authorize the additional eucharistic prayers would lead to a keen disappointment and unauthorized usage in some places, and would mean that the provision of eucharistic prayers for liturgy at the end of the decade would not benefit from any period of monitored and widespread experimental use. These issues raised questions of ecclesiology as well as eucharistic theology.'

Two steps were taken before the newly appointed Commission was able to meet for the first time in October 1996. First, the House of Bishops introduced to the Synod in July the Commission's proposals for the revision of the ASB eucharistic rites, deliberately omitting any text of eucharistic prayers, in the hope that the fact that the revisions were minimal would remove Synod's fear of wholesale change.

Secondly, a process of reflection on underlying issues of eucharistic prayer in regional meetings of Bishops was set in train as preface to a resumed discussion of the issues in the full House in January 1997. There was also a 'fringe meeting' mounted by the newly appointed Commission at the November 1996 General Synod for discussion of background issues with the relatively newly elected Synod which had not been involved in the debates of the preceding two years.

The new Commission put no drafting work in hand until after the January 1997 discussion in the House of Bishops which endorsed the strategy of a Synod debate before texts were submitted.

The Commission's initial thinking indicated

'a total of six modern language Eucharistic Prayers in the liturgical provision for 2000. These would include revised versions of the existing ASB Rite A prayers and two or three new compositions ... Six was probably the upper limit of number of prayers the Bishops would feel able to accept.'

There was also clear preference for

'common texts between all prayers at the opening dialogue, the lead–in to the Sanctus, the dominical words in the institution narrative and the lead–in to the final Amen. Any response other than the opening dialogue needed to be clearly optional (which raised questions about the nature of responses; were they to be repeated acclamations or words which carried the action forward?).'

Of the six, one was 'for use when a substantial number of children are present'. This once again raised questions about drafting prayers targeted at particular 'interest groups'. The provision of a highly responsive eucharistic prayer would be welcomed in some quarters; it was equally clear that the intrusion of responses was strongly resisted in other places. The provision of responses which 'took the action forward' was more difficult if the responses were to be purely optional

---

21 The text of these prayers was published and is still available in Colin Buchanan and Trevor Lloyd (eds), *Six Eucharistic Prayers as Proposed in 1996* (Grove Worship Series 136, Grove Books Ltd, Cambridge, 1996).

(though the congregation might repeat a presidential phrase at key stages of the prayer). There might be wisdom in concentrating responsive elements largely in variable prefaces. It was decided that the revision of the Rite B Eucharistic Prayers would be treated as traditional language variants of the modern language prayers rather than as additions to the six proposed texts.

It was also at the January 1997 House of Bishops meeting that arrangements were put in hand for designating twenty parishes in each diocese for experimental use of draft forms of service. The Commission recognized the importance of making available draft texts of eucharistic prayers in such places as soon as possible. In April 1997 the first drafts came to the full Commission. There was frustration that 'no means had been found of "salvaging" features from the six prayers defeated in General Synod' and also 'that the need to keep the numbers of new drafts to a minimum stifled the Commission's freedom of action to an unfortunate extent'.

In revising the Rite A Eucharistic Prayers, an initial decision was to conflate the first and second prayers, accepting the need to incorporate elements from the second prayer which made it particularly valued by some. There was general acceptance that the third Eucharistic Prayer in Rite A should be proposed more or less unamended. Some doubted whether it was necessary to retain the fourth Eucharistic Prayer in a modern-language form, but it was

> 'judged that, however rarely it might be used in comparison with the others, its Prayer Book resonances and origins meant that it would be "politically" important to keep it in a modern language version.'

At the April 1997 meeting first drafts of four new prayers were used in eucharistic worship, in each case presided over by a member of the Commission closely involved in the drafting. As in all the Commission's work, this made an important contribution to discussing draft texts, even if it might suggest liturgical indigestion to celebrate the eucharist five times in three days!

With a number of drafting changes (responding to points made in the July House of Bishops) the prayers emerging from the April 1997 meeting of the Commission were issued for trial use in the twenty parishes per diocese. By April 1998 there could be some reflection on the texts in the light of actual use.

It was evident from the responses that there was continued demand for *short* eucharistic prayers. Trial use had also shown that many places might consider a choice of six to be too many, but there was such variety between the choice of two or three which each place would favour that it could only be satisfied by making the 'package' of six available. The Commission was determined that there could be no fewer than six offered to the Synod process and would have been prepared to make that publicly known had the House of Bishops declined to forward one or more of the six drafts.

In fact, however, the Bishops agreed to forward six drafts to the synodical process, which began in July 1998. The Chairman of the revision committee was Bishop Christopher Herbert of St Albans (already chairing the revision committee for Rites A and B). The Commission members were David Stancliffe, Jeremy

Haselock, Bishop James Jones of Liverpool and, in the course of the work, the revision committee agreed to co–opt another member of the Commission (Michael Perham), who was on the revision committee on eucharistic rites.[23]

The process extended to the very brink of publishing possibilities if texts were to be published by 1 January 2001, Final Approval being given at the General Synod on 1 March 2000. It is of interest to note, in the light of the earlier process, not least in the House of Bishops, and of the discussions in the Commission, that (including both Orders One and Two) there are now no less than nine modern language eucharistic prayers in *Common Worship*, one of them (Prayer H[24]) being introduced as an entirely new text later than July 1999 in response to persistent demand for a briefer and more responsive text than any others being offered.

Eucharistic Rites

In a preliminary and general discussion in March 1994 the Commission reflected on twenty years' use of ASB and of its predecessors and the growing availability of new eucharistic material which was then under discussion (in conjunction with *A Service of the Word*).

At that early date there was already reflection on

(a) the function of the opening sentence in relation to the Greeting and a need to underscore the presidential nature of the Greeting;

(b) general support for one normative place for penitential material at the beginning, reserving the middle position for occasions of special penitential significance;

(c) stronger encouragement for use of psalmody between lessons and an acclamation before the Gospel;

(d) clearer signals as to when the Creed need not be used and the possibility of alternatives;

(e) careful guidance on the handling of intercession; and

(f) the need to tidy up ambiguities surrounding 'offertory' and 'taking'.

There was a strong concern at that initial stage for there to be greater clarity about roles and functions of various participants in the eucharist (presidential, diaconal etc).[25]

These initial aspirations and hopes for revision of the eucharistic rites in ASB developed into a report for the House of Bishops in January 1996. The proposals were revised at the final meeting of the 1991–96 Commission, discussed again in

---

23 The texts were introduced to the General Synod as GS 1299 and the public record of the process is contained in the Committee Reports: GS 1299Y, GS 1299X and GS 1299W.

24 As well as the official record of Synod debate, attention is drawn to *Common Worship Eucharistic Prayer H: An Unauthorized Account* by Colin Buchanan (Ushaw Library Bulletin and Liturgical Review No.13, September 2000), also available as an offprint from the author.

25 This concern was particularly understandable at that date, when there had evolved significant roles for women deacons who had not, until then, been able to be priested. One member of the Commission (Canon Jane Sinclair) was absent for the second half of the middle day of the Commission's March 1994 meeting because she went to Sheffield to be priested. She presided at the Eucharist for the first time at the Commission's meeting the next day, i.e. on 17 March 1994.

the House of Bishops in June and further tidied by the Chairman and a number of members of the outgoing Commission, so that they could be introduced to the General Synod in July 1996. The new Commission was not able to meet until October 1996, so that the proposals introduced to Synod as GS 1211 were the work of the 1991–96 Commission.

One issue which had been discussed in the Commission and with the House of Bishops was whether or not it was expedient to continue the ASB option of Rite A 'following the pattern of the Book of Common Prayer'. The draft introduced to the Synod did not include such an option but it was evident from submissions to the Revision Committee that it needed to be. Another strand in discussions between the outgoing Commission and House of Bishops had been how best to cater for those wishing to use the BCP 'as used' rather than with the full 1662 text (eg Summary of the Law instead of Commandments, omission of longer Exhortations etc). The House of Bishops encouraged discussion of this issue in the General Synod on the basis of a report (GS Misc 487). The response to that encouraged the revision committee to take that work into its remit after a Synod debate in November 1996.

The revision committee was chaired by Bishop Herbert of St Albans and the Commission members were Michael Perham (co–opted to stay in the Synod after his move to Derby to see this work to completion), Jeremy Haselock and Jane Sinclair. Jeremy Fletcher was an appointed member of the committee, and he became a member of the Commission in the course of the committee's work.

One background factor in the finalizing of the Commission's proposals to the House of Bishops was the availability of the IALC statement on the Eucharist emanating from a meeting in Dublin in August 1995 (*Renewing the Anglican Eucharist,* Grove Worship Series 135).

The reports of the work of the revision committee are in the public domain (GS 1211Y and GS 1211X). From time to time committee members brought issues to the Commission, and there was a celebration of an interim stage of what became Order One as part of the Commission's own worship. One proposal to the revision committee from a Commission member (Trevor Lloyd) was that, as well as Orders One and Two there should, in effect, be an Order Three, which would be an 'outline order' along the lines of the aborted Rite C in the *Patterns for Worship* proposals. Although the proposal did not reach authorization in that precise form, the incorporation of the Outline Structure of each Order into *Common Worship* could be said to go some way towards providing a clear 'pattern' to underpin a celebration of the eucharist, a feature which found its way into other *Common Worship* rites with the Commission's encouragement.

The Commission supported Michael Perham in proposing a detached 'Form of Preparation' incorporating a range of penitential material. The Commission also encouraged no change in the provision already made for 'The Taking', notwithstanding its recommittal for a second revision committee stage. By the time the final shape of the proposals was known (at the Commission's meeting in January 1998) it was noted that the change from Rites A and B to Orders One and Two had made

'a shift, perhaps unconscious, . . . giving an apparent equal weighting to the traditional and Prayer Book "shapes". It had also given prominence to a contemporary language version of the Prayer Book shape which it had not enjoyed whilst it had existed as one option within Rite A.'

After the second revision stage in General Synod in November 1998 the revision of the eucharistic rites was held back from Final Approval until February 2000 so that the agreed texts of the eucharistic prayers could be known at the time that Final Approval was given. But in fact delay was needed because the House of Bishops met unforeseen difficulty in reaching an agreed text of the Nicene Creed.

Nicene Creed

One thorny matter of disagreement in the Revision Committee, which fell to the House of Bishops to determine (as a doctrinal matter) was the translation of the Nicene Creed. Before determining the text to be returned to Synod for Final Approval that House staged no fewer than three debates on the issue (on the basis of a Report, GS 1535). The matter for protracted debate at that late stage was the wording of the line which refers to the action of the Holy Spirit and the role of the Virgin Mary in the incarnation. It finally emerged as 'was incarnate from the Holy Spirit and the Virgin Mary.' There were, however, other issues connected with the Nicene Creed which had been debated at an earlier stage — the *Filioque* clause, and also retention of 'man' in the line 'and was made man', where the internationally and ecumenically agreed text of the Nicene Creed published by ELLC had recommended 'and became truly human'. The Synod had been asked to decide whether the ELLC phrase (judged to be inelegant English, even if theologically irreproachable) should be incorporated in liturgical revision or whether the more familiar 'and was made man' should be retained. That decision had been taken in the context of the debate on *Language and the Worship of the Church* in July 1994 and it fell to members of the Commission to keep the implications of that decision alive in subsequent discussions, particularly when the incarnation section of the Nicene Creed came under close scrutiny in 1999.

A Private Member's Motion in the early 1990s had called for the omission of the *Filioque* clause from the Nicene Creed at the next round of liturgical revision. Synod then resolved that the *Filioque* clause would be retained in the text of the Nicene Creed within the main eucharistic rite, but that a text without the *Filioque* clause for use on appropriate ecumenical occasions would be printed somewhere in the book which replaced the ASB after 2000. In the years after 1994 the Commission, through its members serving on the appropriate revision committee and on the publishing committee, had to draw attention to the implications of that decision. The process neatly illustrates the interaction between liturgy and doctrine and the controlling role of the House of Bishops.

41

Public Worship with Communion by Extension

One of the most controversial and theologically divisive issues in this period was whether authorized provision should be made for a service at which elements consecrated at a Eucharist in another church might be distributed to the congregation. So sharp were the divisions that it was unclear until the Final Approval vote in July 2000 whether it would be authorized (when the two-thirds majority in the House of Laity was attained by 131–64). However the Commission's responsibility was to provide liturgical drafts for the proposal once the House of Bishops decided to address the issue. The need for synodical authorization stemmed partly from a legal ruling that provision for the distribution of eucharistic elements was probably alternative to a provision in the Book of Common Prayer. Although its progress through General Synod was under the guise of liturgical business the issue was decidedly 'led' by the House of Bishops, seeking to make a sensitive pastoral provision requiring carefully–nuanced liturgical text.

The Commission discussed this for the first time in September 1991, in the context of a copyright application from a diocese seeking permission for such a rite. The Commission took the view that the principles involved should be considered by the House of Bishops. The matter was remitted to the Theological Group of the House of Bishops and by May 1992 that group was seeking draft texts. The Commission was clear that:

(a) Reservation for such use should be in both kinds;

(b) The Eucharist where the elements were consecrated should involve prayer for the congregation receiving the elements at a subsequent service;

(c) The wording and choreography should make clear that no full celebration of the Eucharist was taking place, with rubrics positioning the minister well away from the Holy Table for as much of the rite as was physically possible; and

(d) Opportunity should be taken to discourage the (then) widespread practice of 'deacons in charge' presiding for all but the narrative of institution within the eucharistic prayer, spoken by a visiting priest.

The Commission was also concerned that adequate guidance should be available; urging the bishops to think who should be authorized to conduct the rite; agreed that the rite should explicitly preclude the possibility of adding more bread or wine should the consecrated elements be used up before all those present had communicated and aware that there would need to be a BCP form since the provision might be expected to be used in rural situations where the Prayer Book was the customary use. There was also discussion about how to incorporate thanksgiving without any possibility of misunderstanding that it constituted a eucharistic prayer and about the need to keep discussion of the issue distinct from the practice of reservation for the purposes of communicating the sick.

A Synod debate (on a 'take note' motion) took place in November 1993 with the Commission's draft rite appended as 'illustration' of the sort of provision that could be made if the practice were to be approved. It was clear from the debate that fundamental issues (including that of 'lay presidency') had been raised, and that no further work would be appropriate until these wider issues had been considered by the House of Bishops, after a period of more public discussion led by them.

In summer 1995 the House of Bishops declared its intention of introducing the Commission's draft rite to the Synod. The Commission proposed that notes relating to the occasions for use and persons who might officiate should be included in the rite (and so be authorized), rather than in the (less authoritative) guidelines which the Bishops had now produced.

The draft was introduced to General Synod (November 1997) and began the most fragmented of the processes in the 1990s. The General Approval debate was itself divided between two meetings of Synod and only remitted to a revision committee after a vote by Houses in February 1998. Bishop Peter Forster of Chester chaired the revision committee, with Jeremy Haselock, Anna de Lange and Timothy Slater in the committee from the Commission. The work of the revision committee did not conclude until July 1999 (GS 1230Y and GS 1230X) since the matter was referred to a second revision committee stage. It was decided that it would be published as an appendix to bishops' guidelines rather than as part of the 'mainstream' liturgy in *Common Worship*, so there was no pressing need to meet the publication deadline, and Final Approval came in July 2000. This rite is unique as a fully authorized liturgy in the Church of England, alternative to the provision of the Book of Common Prayer, which is only available for use in a diocese if the bishop gives express permission for it to be used. There are currently some dioceses where it is used and others where it is not.

The Ordinal

In 1999 and 2000 synodical processes extended the use of the ASB Ordinal for five years to 31 December 2005, subject to 'minor adjustments of its text to bring it into line with *Common Worship* forms'. The text of a proposed revision of the Ordinal was brought to the Synod in February 2004, with the hope of Final Approval in time for 2006.

The work of the current Commission builds on the foundation of extended reflection on issues connected with ordination. IALC took three meetings (1997, 1999 and 2001) preparing a statement on ordination liturgy.[26] In 1997 preliminary discussion in the Commission on possible changes in the structure of the ASB rite to bring it into closer line with primitive practice and the fruits of recent scholarship, centred on the place in the rite for the presentation and the giving of the Bible and symbols of Order, the involvement (at the presentation) of

26 The Commission provided material for the House of Bishops on appropriate adaptation of the Ordinal for women deacons (1983), and priests (1993). In 1988 Lambeth sought the Commission's advice on the practice of laying hands in episcopal ordinations, where the English bishops laid hands together but visiting bishops followed with individual layings–on of hands, after Roman Catholic and Old Catholic practice. The Commission said visiting bishops ought to lay on hands exactly the same way as English bishops—whether simultaneous or serial—though in March 1994 the Commission thought there might be a case for re–examining the appropriateness of 'the scrum'.

representatives from the local congregation and the training process, the closer identification of the prayers of the people with the ordination prayer, and modification of the hand-laying practice to identify it more clearly with the whole ordination prayer rather than it being seen as a 'formula' between two prayers.

A first engagement with the House of Bishops in January 1998 provided an opportunity for bishops to compare practice and to recognize the implications different practices implied in interpretation. Work involving the House of Bishops' Theological Group and the Faith and Order Advisory Group was initiated and a book of essays on background issues was mooted.

There were further wide–ranging discussion at the Commission's meetings in October and December 1998 in preparation for the House of Bishops in January 1999. A collation of ordination practice across all dioceses of the Church of England in June 1999 disclosed widely varying practice and custom to an extent which had not hitherto been appreciated. The Commission held consultations with representatives of the Ministry Division and Principals of Colleges and Courses in July 2000 and with representatives of the Faith and Order Advisory Group and the Council for Christian Unity in December 2000.

This Study has described how the essential components of Common Worship to replace the ASB were in place by December 2000 and indicates how the project as a whole will be complete by 2005.

Appendix:
Membership of the Liturgical Commission from 1981

1981-1986
The Revd Professor Canon D R Jones (Chairman); The Revd Dr Paul Bradshaw; The Revd Canon Colin Buchanan; The Revd Dr Donald Gray; The Revd Canon Colin Hickling; The Revd Dr David Hope; The Revd Trevor Lloyd; The Revd Graham Midgley; Deaconess Diana McClatchey; The Revd Dr Geoffrey Rowell; The Rt Revd Richard Rutt, Bishop of Leicester; The Venerable David Silk; The Rt Revd John Taylor, Bishop of St Albans; Miss Jinny Wade; Mrs Ann Warren; The Revd Canon Hugh Wybrew; Consultants: The Revd Canon Dr Geoffrey Cuming; The Revd Michael Perham; Mr Robin Brookes.

1986-1991
The Rt Revd Colin James, Bishop of Winchester (Chairman); The Rt Revd Michael Baughen, Bishop of Chester (resigned 1987); The Revd Dr Mark Dalby; Mrs Molly Dow (from 1987); The Venerable Trevor Lloyd; The Revd Michael Perham; The Rt Revd William Persson, Bishop of Doncaster (from 1987); The Revd Dr Geoffrey Rowell; Mr Adrian Scott (resigned 1987); The Venerable David Silk; The Revd Jane Sinclair; The Revd Dr Bryan Spinks; The Very Revd David Stancliffe, Provost of Portsmouth; The Revd Dr Kenneth Stevenson; The Revd Canon John Sweet; The Revd Michael Vasey; Miss Jinny Wade; Consultants: The Revd Canon Dr Donald Gray; Mr Robin Brookes.

1991-1996
The Rt Revd Colin James, Bishop of Winchester (Chairman to 1993); The Rt Revd David Stancliffe, Bishop of Salisbury (Chairman from 1993); The Venerable Dr Mark Dalby; Mrs Molly Dow; The Revd Canon Roger Greenacre; The Rt Revd Patrick Harris, Bishop of Southwell; The Baroness James of Holland Park; The Venerable Trevor Lloyd; The Revd Stephen Oliver; The Revd Canon Michael Perham; The Revd Canon Jane Sinclair; The Revd Dr Bryan Spinks; The Revd Dr Kenneth Stevenson; The Revd Canon Dr John Sweet; The Revd Michael Vasey; Dr Susan White (to February 1995); The Very Revd Robert Willis (from June 1995); Consultants: The Revd Canon Dr Donald Gray; Brother Tristam SSF (to 1995, when he became a member); Roman Catholic Observer: The Revd Geoffrey Steel.

1996-2001
The Rt Revd David Stancliffe, Bishop of Salisbury (Chairman); The Revd Andrew Burnham; The Revd Dr Christopher Cocksworth; Dr Carole Cull; Mrs Anna de Lange; The Revd Jeremy Fletcher (from 1998); The Revd Canon Jeremy Haselock;

The Revd Sue Hope; The Baroness James of Holland Park; The Rt Revd James Jones, Bishop of Hull, later Liverpool; The Venerable Trevor Lloyd; The Revd Canon Stephen Oliver; The Very Revd Michael Perham, Provost (later Dean) of Derby; The Revd Canon Jane Sinclair; Mr Tim Slater; The Revd Angela Tilby (from 1998); Brother Tristam SSF; The Revd Michael Vasey (to 1998); The Very Revd Robert Willis (to 1997); Consultants: The Revd Canon Dr John Sweet (to 1997); The Revd Canon Dr Anders Bergquist (from 1997); The Revd Professor Dr Bryan Spinks; The Revd Professor Dr Paul Bradshaw; The Rt Revd Dr Kenneth Stevenson, Bishop of Portsmouth; Roman Catholic Observer: The Revd Geoffrey Steel.

2001 onwards
The Rt Revd David Stancliffe, Bishop of Salisbury (Chairman); Mrs Angela Ashwin (to 2002); The Rt Revd Colin Bennetts, Bishop of Coventry; The Revd Canon Dr Anders Bergquist; The Revd Mark Bonney; The Revd Professor Dr Paul Bradshaw; The Revd Dr Christopher Cocksworth; The Revd Peter Craig-Wild; Ms Dana Delap; The Revd Canon Jeremy Fletcher; The Revd Canon Jeremy Haselock; The Rt Revd Christopher Hill, Bishop of Stafford (from 2003); Mrs Sarah James; The Revd Canon Dr David Kennedy; The Revd Canon Dr Graham Kings; The Revd Canon George Kovoor; The Revd Dr Paul Roberts; The Revd Angela Tilby; Brother Tristam SSF (to 2002); Consultants: The Revd Professor John Barton; The Rt Revd Andrew Burnham, Bishop of Ebbsfleet; The Revd Dr Anne Dawtry; The Revd Dr Anthony Gelston; Professor Dr John Harper; The Venerable Trevor Lloyd (to 2002); The Rt Revd Dr Kenneth Stevenson, Bishop of Portsmouth; Observers: The Revd Dr Kenneth Carveley (Methodist); The Revd Allen Morris (Roman Catholic); The Revd Gilly Myers (Secretary of *Praxis*).

These lists do not include staff members in attendance, notably from 1999-2000 the Revd Mark Earey, *Praxis* National Education Officer. Prior to 1996 the Secretary was almost invariably the only staff member present.

THE GROUP FOR RENEWAL OF WORSHIP (GROW)

This Group, originally founded in 1961, has for thirty years taken responsibility for the Grove Books publications on liturgy and worship. Its membership and broad aims reflect a highly reforming, pastoral and missionary interest in worship. Beginning with a youthful evangelical Anglican membership in the early 1970s, the Group has not only probed adventurously into the future of Anglican worship, but has also with growing sureness of touch taken its place in promoting weighty scholarship. Thus the 'Grove Liturgical Studies' over a twelve-year period from 1975 to 1986 added steadily to the material available to students of patristic, reformation and modern scholarly issues in liturgy. Many of these are still in print and available from Grove Books Ltd. In 1986 the Group was approached by the Alcuin Club Committee with a view to publishing the new series of Joint Liturgical Studies, and this series is, at the time of writing, in its eighteenth year of publication, sustaining the programme until 2002 with three Studies each year. From 2003 the studies are reduced to two each year.

Between the old Grove Liturgical Studies and the new Joint Liturgical Studies there is a large provision of both English language texts and other theological works on the patristic era. A detailed consolidated list is available from the publishers.

THE ALCUIN CLUB

The Alcuin Club exists to promote the study of Christian liturgy in general, and in particular the liturgies of the Anglican Communion. Since its foundation in 1897 it has published over 130 books and pamphlets. Members of the Club receive some publications of the current year free and others at a reduced rate.

Information concerning the annual subscription, applications for membership and lists of publications is obtainable from the Treasurer, The Revd. T. R. Barker, The Parsonage, 8 Church Street, Spalding, Lincs. PE11 2 PB. (Tel. 01775 722675).

The Alcuin Club has worked with a number of publishers in the UK and the USA to publish a major work of liturgical scholarship every year. Recent books include *Make Music to Our God* (Reginald Box SSF), *The Rites of Christian Initiation: Their Evolution and Interpretation* (Maxwell Johnson), *Daily Prayer in Christian Spain: A Study of the Mozarabic Office* (Graham Woolfenden) and *A Companion to Common Worship, volume 1* (edited by Paul Bradsahw).

In 2002, Alcuin and SPCK published two Liturgical Guides—on art and worship (Christopher Irvine and Anne Dawtry) and memorial services (Donald Gray).

The Alcuin Club's annual subscription entitles members to receive, without further charge, the two Joint Liturgical Studies and the Club's major annual publication. Occasionally, further books are offered to members at discounted prices.

Alcuin/GROW Joint Liturgical Studies

All cost £4.95 (US $8) in 2004 — nos. 4 and 16 are out of print

1. **(LS 49) Daily and Weekly Worship — from Jewish to Christian** by Roger Beckwith
2. **(LS 50) The Canons of Hippolytus** edited by Paul Bradshaw
3. **(LS 51) Modern Anglican Ordination Rites** edited by Colin Buchanan
5. **(LS 53) A Kingdom of Priests: Liturgical Formation of the Laity: The Brixen Essays** edited by Thomas Talley
6. **(LS 54) The Bishop in Liturgy: an Anglican Study** edited by Colin Buchanan
7. **(LS 55) Inculturation: the Eucharist in Africa** by Phillip Tovey
8. **(LS 56) Essays in Early Eastern Initiation** edited by Paul Bradshaw,
9. **(LS 57) The Liturgy of the Church in Jerusalem** by John Baldovin
10. **(LS 58) Adult Initiation** edited by Donald Withey
11. **(LS 59) 'The Missing Oblation': The Contents of the Early Antiochene Anaphora** by John Fenwick
12. **(LS 60) Calvin and Bullinger on the Lord's Supper** by Paul Rorem
13-14 **(LS 61) The Liturgical Portions of the Apostolic Constitutions: A Text for Students** edited by W. Jardine Grisbrooke (This double-size volume costs double price (i.e. £9.90))
15 **(LS 62) Liturgical Inculturation in the Anglican Communion** edited by David Holeton
17. **(LS 64) The Preaching Service — The Glory of the Methodists** by Adrian Burdon
18. **(LS 65) Irenaeus of Lyon on Baptism and Eucharist** edited with Introduction, Translation and Commentary by David Power
19. **(LS 66) Testamentum Domini** edited by Grant Sperry-White
20. **(LS 67) The Origins of the Roman Rite** edited by Gordon Jeanes
21. **The Anglican Eucharist in New Zealand 1814-1989** by Bosco Peters
22-23 **Foundations of Christian Music: The Music of Pre-Constantinian Christianity** by Edward Foley (double-sized volume at £9.90)
24. **Liturgical Presidency** by Paul James
25. **The Sacramentary of Sarapion of Thmuis: A Text for Students** edited by Ric Lennard-Barrett
26. **Communion Outside the Eucharist** by Phillip Tovey
27. **Revising the Eucharist: Groundwork for the Anglican Communion** edited by David Holeton
28. **Anglican Liturgical Inculturation in Africa** edited by David Gitari
29-30. **On Baptismal Fonts: Ancient and Modern** by Anita Stauffer (double-sized volume at £9.90)
31. **The Comparative Liturgy of Anton Baumstark** by Fritz West
32. **Worship and Evangelism in Pre-Christendom** by Alan Kreider
33. **Liturgy in Early Christian Egypt** by Maxwell E. Johnson
34. **Welcoming the Baptized** by Timothy Turner
35. **Daily Prayer in the Reformed Tradition: An Initial Survey** by Diane Karay Tripp
36. **The Ritual Kiss in Early Christian Worship** by Edward Phillips
37. **'After the Primitive Christians': The Eighteenth-century Anglican Eucharist in its Architectural Setting** by Peter Doll
38. **Coronations Past, Present and Future** edited by Paul Bradshaw
39. **Anglican Orders and Ordinations** edited by David Holeton
40. **The Liturgy of St James as presently used** edited by Phillip Tovey
41. **Anglican Missals** by Mark Dalby
42. **The Origins of the Roman Rite vol 2** edited by Gordon Jeanes
43. **Baptism in Early Byzantine Palestine 325-451** by Juliette Day
44. **Ambrosianum Mysterium: the Church of Milan and its Liturgical Tradition Vol. 1** by Cesare Alzati (translated by George Guiver)
45. **Mar Nestorius and Mar Theodore the Interpreter: the forgotten Eucharistic Prayers of East Syria** edited by Bryan Spinks
46. **The Eucharistic Theology of the Later Nonjurors** by James Smith
47-48. **Ambrosianum Mysterium: the Church of Milan and its Liturgical Tradition Vol. II** by Cesare Alzati (translated by George Guiver) (double-sized volume at £9.90)
49. **The Syriac Version of the Liturgy of St James: A brief history for Students** by Dr Baby Varghese
50. **Offerings from Kenya to Anglicanism: Liturgical Texts and Contexts including 'A Kenyan Service of Holy Communion'** by Graham Kings and Geoff Morgan
51. **Early Jewish Liturgy: A Source Book for use by Students of Early Christian Liturgy** edited and translated by Alistair Stewart-Sykes and Judith H Newman
52. **Church and Worship in Fifth-Century Rome: The Letter of Innocent I to Decentius of Gubbio** by Martin F Connell
53. **Public Worship and Communion by Extension: some Pastoral and Theological Issues** by Alex Hughes
54. **The Savoy Conference Revisited** by Colin Buchanan
55. **Sequential or Direct Ordination? A return to the Sources** by John St. H. Gibaut
56. **Infant Communion — The New Testament to the Reformation** by Mark Dalby
57. **Liturgical Revision in the Church of England 1984-2004: The Working of the Liturgical Commission** by David Hebblethwaite